Building A Financial Fortress

Lessons from the Great Recession for Savers and Investors

By Nick Reichert

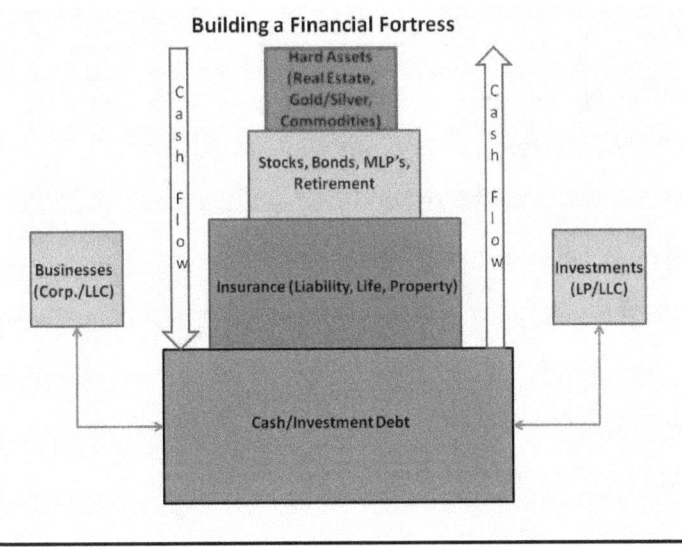

Building a Financial Fortress

Building A Financial Fortress

Contents

Foreword

I have always been interested in personal financial planning since first starting my career in the accounting field 23 years ago. In that time working as a Certified Public Accountant and later in the real estate development business, I have seen many market cycles and have struggled with how to manage my investments and protect my wealth.

This book is a re-publication of a blog I started in the depths of the Great Recession in March 2011. During that time, as I agonized over investing, saving and potential job loss, I developed an investment philosophy I dubbed the "Financial Fortress" and wrote a series of posts about it along with other posts about specific asset classes, investment strategies and related topics.

My two biggest successes have been in real estate and precious metals. During the Great Recession, I made some aggressive moves, using retirement savings, to purchase distressed condominiums in Orange County, California. In addition to enjoying positive cash flow while I owned the properties, I have just completed one sale and have a second one in escrow, doubling my money in five years. I also made an aggressive move into silver (US Silver Eagle coins) to watch them triple in value, at which time I sold individual rolls on EBay and kept the rest for future appreciation.

The essence of the Financial Fortress is that as savers and investors, we need to first have a strong defense before we can have a strong offense. As volatility in world markets seems to worsen each year and booms/busts become more intense, preservation of capital is paramount but so is finding opportunities to leverage what we have in order to grow our wealth.

I have found the keys to success are:

- Education
- Contrarian thinking
- Flexibility/willingness to consider other alternatives
- Where there's a will, there's a way

Building A Financial Fortress

I hope this book will give you some ideas on how you can protect and grow your own wealth.

Regards,

Nick Reichert

Connect:

Twitter - @NickReichert

Facebook - https://www.facebook.com/BuildingAFinancialFortress

Website – http://www.buildingafinancialfortress.com

Pinterest - http://www.pinterest.com/nickreichert1

Chapter 1 - How To Build A Financial Fortress

2012-09-08

You can visualize your personal finances as a fortress. A fortress offers you protection and peace of mind from the vagaries of the stock/bond market, the economy, worries about retirement or funding children's educations, life's unexpected expenses, etc.

The graphic on the next page depicts the Financial Fortress:

Building A Financial Fortress

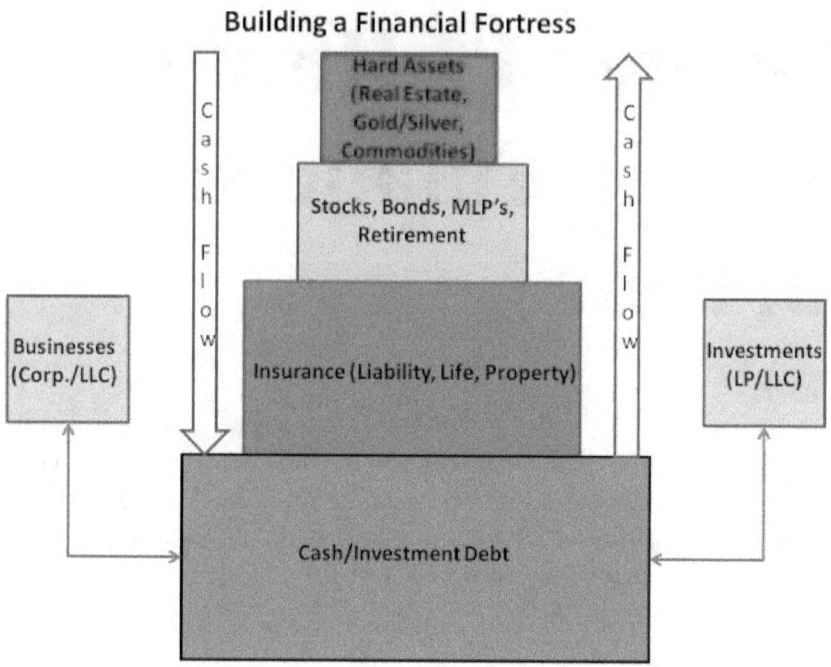

Building a Financial Fortress

The Financial Fortress has 5 components as follows:

1. **Cash/Investment Debt** forms the base. Adequate levels of cash are needed to protect against uncertainties and for new investment opportunities. Investment debt ("good debt") allows leverage (other people's money) to buy assets that will generate additional positive cash flow - i.e., a mortgage for an investment property or a personal loan to start a business or make a new investment. "Bad debt" like credit card debt, auto loans, etc. should be paid off as soon as possible. If you have cash earning 0.5% or less in a bank, you can't afford not to pay off "bad debt."

2. **Insurance (Liability, Life and Property)** - form the next layer. Insurance provides protection against accidents or lawsuits and also protects your real and personal property in the event of a loss. Life insurance protects your family in the event of death and also provides a nice retirement planning vehicle.

3. **Businesses and Investments** form the two components that are outside the fortress; these are like watchtowers, places where you can conduct

a business or outside investment with other investors, but they are isolated from the main fortress for liability reasons; these will typically be held in limited liability entities, such as corporations, LLC's, LP's, etc. Everyone should have a business, even (and especially) if they work at a regular job - something you are passionate about that has the potential to make money. You never know, you may need to quit your day job to run your business! What business are you in?

4. **Stocks, Bonds, MLP's and Retirement** - form the next component of the fortress. This is where paper assets, including stocks, bonds, master limited partnerships (which are excellent sources of cash flow with commodity upside); 401(k) and IRA accounts are held. The taxable stocks that pay dividends and bonds provide a source of positive cash flow to replenish the base of the Financial Fortress.

5. **Hard Assets (Real Estate, Gold/Silver, Commodities)** form the top of the fortress. These assets provide long term protection against inflation and in the case of real estate and some commodities, a steady source of positive cash flow to replenish the base of the Financial Fortress.

Poverty is often concealed in splendor, and often in extravagance. It is the task of many people to conceal their neediness from others. Consequently they support themselves by temporary means, and every day is lost in contriving for tomorrow.

Samuel Johnson – Poverty, extravagance

US Unemployment Rate and Investment Implications

2012-07-06

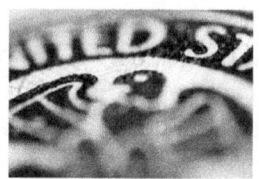

The United States unemployment rate remains at an elevated level, the result of very slow job growth, as shown in the chart below. While the headline news is disappointing (80,000 non-farm jobs added and 8.2% unemployment), there has been positive employment growth for the past two years. Unfortunately, the job growth just hasn't been strong enough to replace all the jobs that were lost in the Great Recession. Depending on what happens in Europe and China, and also depending on the Federal Reserve's policy response, there's a good chance that the US could slip back into recession within the next year.

Building A Financial Fortress

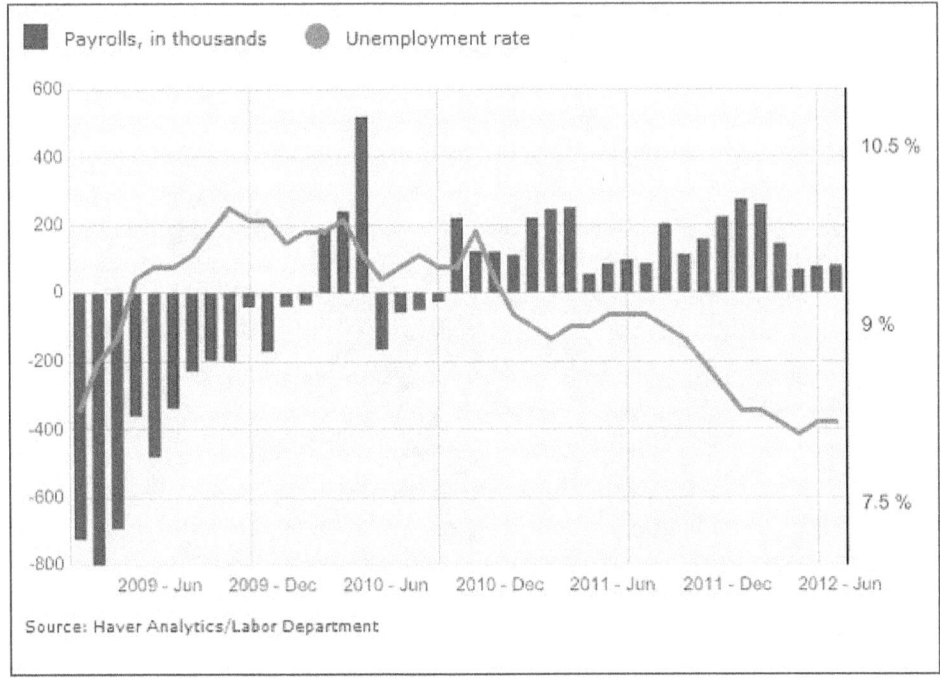

Payrolls, in thousands ● Unemployment rate

Source: Haver Analytics/Labor Department

Most of the major developed economies are dealing with elevated rates of unemployment, as shown in the chart below. The United States is about average for this group (Japan is the best at about 4% and France/Italy are the worst at about 10%). Interestingly, France is planning a big tax increase to close its budget gap, which will only make their situation worse, since tax increases tend to stifle economic activity. Similarly, in the United States, if the Bush tax cuts are allowed to expire at the end of 2012, this is expected to hurt economic growth in the United States and could be the necessary catalyst to put the US back into recession.

Building A Financial Fortress

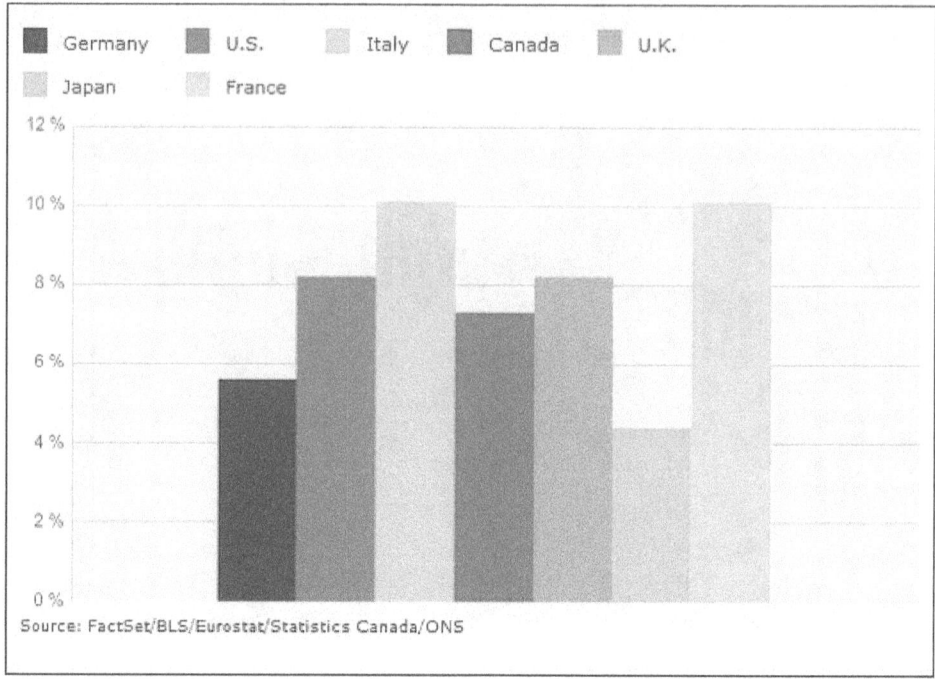

It appears that the "new normal" theory, marked by delevering, deglobalization and reregulation and associated slow economic growth continues to help explain what is happening. Clearly, central bank interest rate policies have been the major factor in the upward movements in both stock and bond markets recently and also a major reason why real estate has stabilized. When global investors are in panic mode, as they have been recently, they flock to short-term Treasuries and the US dollar and sell just about everything else.

What is the right investment approach for the current environment?

1. Cash is king, but not too much; you want to stay liquid in order to take advantage of buying opportunities and also to make sure you have reserves for safety, however low short term rates and inflation will hurt over the longer term
2. Be careful with bonds - keep the duration short; long term bond yields may look attractive but they will get hammered when interest rates rise

Building A Financial Fortress

3. If you are in the stock market, make sure you have trading stops or other types of hedges, such as inverse Exchange Traded Funds to protect your portfolio; otherwise, sell now before that bubble bursts
4. Buy physical gold and silver on dips and hang on - with the entire world printing money now to re-inflate economies and bail out banks, the long term outlook for precious metals is excellent even if there is some short-term volatility
5. Buy an investment property (4 units or less) and take advantage of the generous, government subsidized 30 year fixed rate financing that is available; just make sure the property is cash flow positive - owning a rental property is looking better and better as rents continue to increase throughout the US

Quote of the Day - Steve Martin on Wealth

2012-09-07

"If you've got a dollar and you spend 29 cents on a loaf of bread, you've got 71 cents left; But if you've got seventeen grand and you spend 29 cents on a loaf of bread, you've still got seventeen grand. There's a math lesson for you."
— Steve Martin

What is the True Meaning of "Diversified Investment Portfolio?"

2012-08-19

You have probably heard for years from investment advisors, the media, your stockbroker, friends, and family that your investments should be diversified. In 2008, you probably learned that diversification across a broad array of stocks and stock mutual funds doesn't help you if the entire stock market craters at the same time. Lately, it seems that mutual fund investors are moving away from the stock market back into bonds for "safety," but what happens if/when the bond market craters? Timing the market is notoriously difficult to do and yet it seems like investors today are embracing market timing more than ever because the "buy and hold" mantra is no longer believable. You just have to look at the stock market over the past 5 years to see that the winners are the ones who bought at the bottom in early 2009 and are now enjoying the run-up - just waiting for the right time to sell. Investors who are still holding since 2008 (if there are any) are still looking at a loss.

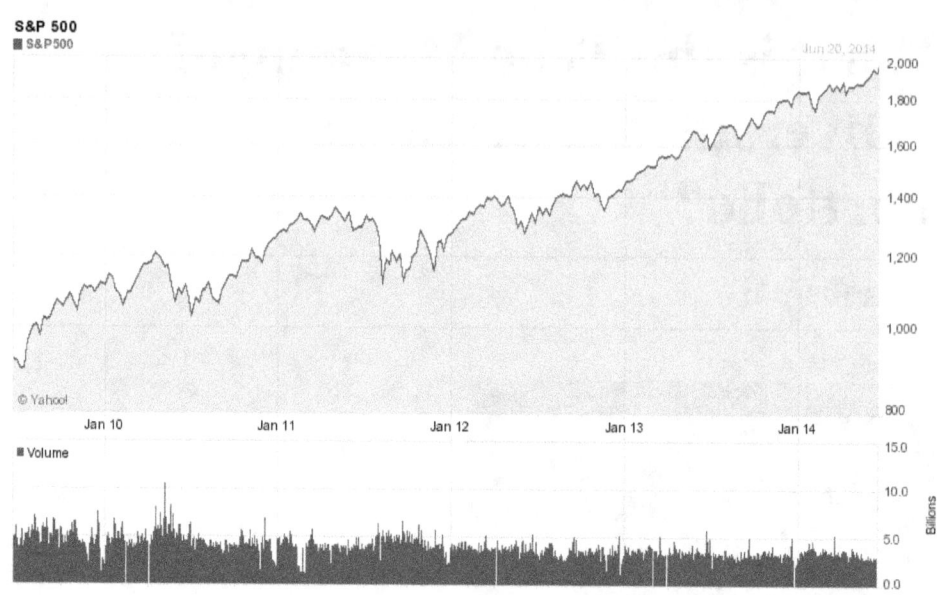

Diversification isn't about having a bunch of different stocks or bonds or mutual funds that invest in stocks and bonds. It's also not about market timing or picking a winner. It's really about making sure that you can make money in any market situation and not lose 30%-50% or more of the value of your portfolio in a bad market stretch. Having all of your money in cash is also troubling given the fact that as much as everyone wants to believe it's not true, the value of the dollar is declining every day and there is real inflation out there, even if the official Consumer Price Index measure isn't showing it..

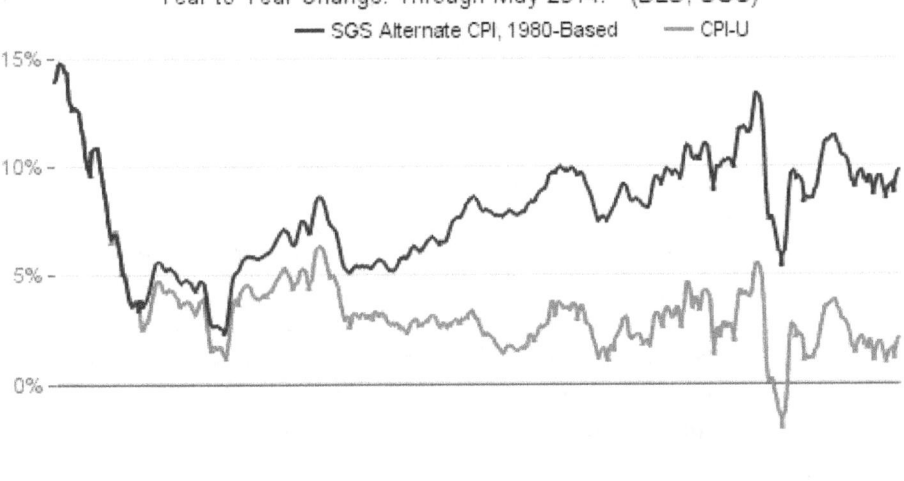

Consumer Inflation - Official vs ShadowStats (1980-Based) Alternate
Year to Year Change. Through May 2014. (BLS, SGS)
—— SGS Alternate CPI, 1980-Based   —— CPI-U

Published: June 17, 2014   shadowstats.com

What would a prudent investor do, then, to protect themselves by using diversification properly? Here's a sample investment strategy that would meet these objectives in today's investment environment:

- Stocks - 20%
    - Include international, domestic, emerging markets - some of these are really beaten down now, especially Europe and emerging markets (caution: may not have seen the bottom, yet)
    - Index funds should be part of the mix - low cost
    - ETF's are better than mutual funds, especially for 401(k) accounts if available
    - Don't be afraid to pick one or two good companies and hold on to them - Warren Buffett has done pretty well with that strategy over the years
- Bonds - 20%

- o Pick a good bond manager with a good track record - I like PIMCO or BlackRock, unless you want to do all the research and evaluate credit quality of issuers
- o Include different sub-markets - municipal bonds, Treasuries and corporate bonds, including some high yield exposure
- Real Estate - 20%
  - o Feels like a good buy now, especially with historically low interest rates
  - o Investment property - positive cash flow; moderate leverage (70% to 75%)
  - o Better to own directly if possible vs. owning shares in a REIT that can go up and down with the stock market, plus you have control over the asset and business
  - o Requires some time to manage as a business, but also has tax benefits
- Alternative Investments - 20%
  - o Silver, gold or platinum - physical coins or bars are better than ETF's for this category, in my opinion
  - o Shares of mining companies are interesting, but you still have business risk and also general stock market risk in the event of a correction
  - o Oil and gas master limited partnerships offer high current income yields (6% - 8% or higher) with commodity upside (downside is usually hedged - some MLP's are better than others at this) - pipeline MLP's offer yield but minimal commodity risk if that interests you
- Cash - 20%
  - o High yield savings, short-term commercial paper can offer attractive yields
  - o Keep some FDIC-insured accounts just in case

I wouldn't advise making any major moves into the stock or the bond market at this time, due to the high valuations and perceived level of risk. Averaging in over time to hit these targets would make the most sense so you can take advantage of market pullbacks, which are sure to continue, driven by the US election cycle, economic news and the situation in Europe. I feel better about current Real Estate and Alternative Investment valuations and would be a little more aggressive in diversifying into these categories at the present time.

Stay Diversified - Resist Temptation

2013-04-06

Volatility returned to the markets this week with the US employment situation showing weakness, turning investors to bonds again for safety and resulting in a minor sell-off in the stock market.

Again the best strategy seems to be a broadly diversified portfolio with no more than 20% in any one asset class (bonds, stocks, real estate, precious metals and cash).

I prefer not to worry about what's happening from day to day in the markets - trading is very difficult to do, even for those who are professionals.

Debt is the new currency, so leverage as much as you can in real estate while ensuring you have positive cash flow. I'm not a fan of leverage in situations where you can't cover the debt service with the cash flow from the asset. Leveraged investments in precious metals, for example, only work out if the

Building A Financial Fortress

underlying asset skyrockets in value and you sell your position. I much prefer leverage in real estate investments.

Lately, it has been very tempting to sell bonds, increase investments in stocks and real estate and minimize cash holdings. It is important to resist the temptation and stay diversified. At least this way if you suffer a loss in a particular asset class, you won't lose a large percentage of your portfolio.

I believe we are in a perpetual cycle of booms and busts that are driven by credit expansion. Each one is successively worse than the one before. I fear that the next boom and bust will be far worse than the "Great Recession" that we just experienced and indeed many still experience due to high unemployment and destruction of wealth that persist. This is why I favor a diversified approach and also lean toward hard assets (gold, silver, oil/gas real estate) versus financial assets (stocks, bonds, mutual funds) to protect and grow wealth, particularly when we are facing the threat of inflation - a consequence of global central back "easy money" policies.

20 Things You Can Do to Weather the Next Big Financial Crisis

2012-07-15

Here are 20 ideas on preparing for the next big financial crisis, which could be upon us in the next year or two. With the US economy struggling to recover, Europe in shambles and emerging markets also in decline as the world's central banks print money to bail out banks and try to revive economies, I hope I'm wrong, but it makes sense to prepare. These are in no particular order and you might want to act on these ideas even if everything ends up being okay:

1. **Emergency Fund** - If you haven't already done so, build that emergency fund (3 - 6 months of living expenses); keep it in cash in an FDIC insured bank account - remember that in times of crisis, money market funds can "break the buck" and you could lose your principal
2. **Avoid the Stock Market** - If you are in the stock market, sell now; if you aren't, stay out - the only reason the stock market is performing well this year is because of money printing and cheap credit - it's certainly not because of the economy
3. **Use Caution When Investing in Bonds** - If you have to invest in bonds, make sure they are US Treasury securities and the maturity is short - be prepared to pay the US government to hold your money for you, because what you earn won't keep up with inflation; you can buy direct at http://www.treasurydirect.gov/
4. **Gold and Silver** - Buy some physical gold and silver - I personally like the gold buffalo and silver eagle bullion coins produced by the US Mint, they are available from most coin dealers and you can easily follow the price on EBay; when you get them, put them in a bank safe deposit box - some are calling for gold to go up significantly in the next few years (but short-term, it will probably decline due to the temporarily strong dollar and panic selling)

5. **Get/Keep Your Job** - If you have a job, keep it and do the best work you can so you aren't the first one to be laid off. If you don't have a job, get one quick - if you need to, change careers and/or go back to school

6. **Start a Side Business** - Build a business (or two) on the side in your spare time that could become your primary activity in the event you lose your job (always have a Plan "B"); the best time to build it is when you don't have the pressure of having it make money

7. **Pay off Credit Cards** - If you don't have the cash to pay off credit cards, then you can at least consolidate them - Prosper.com is a peer-to-peer lending site that allows you to borrow up to $25,000 at a fixed rate to be repaid over 3-5 years - the lenders are individuals just like you

8. **Think Safety in Your IRA or 401(k)** - Move everything to cash and wait patiently for the market to correct; you really can't afford to lose another 30% to 50%, can you?

9. **Refinance Your Mortgage** - If you haven't done so already, you should refinance your mortgage now - with the new HARP 2 program, you don't have to meet income requirements and there's no appraisal - your loan just needs to be owned by Fannie Mae or Freddie Mac and it needs to meet a few other criteria - follow this link to check; if you have a jumbo loan, you'll have to wait and see or do a short sale (see #12 below)

10. **Make Sure You Have Good, Portable Life Insurance** - What's the worst thing that could happen to you - you lose your job (and with it your employer-provided term life coverage), you get sick and then you die, leaving your family nothing; the easiest way to avoid that is to purchase a whole life or term life policy outside of the workplace with a highly rated insurance company; I prefer mutual life insurance companies like Northwestern Mutual Life, since they are run more for the benefit of policy holders (it is also a highly-rated company); also a whole life policy can supplement your retirement income by providing tax-free withdrawals from the cash surrender value via policy loans; follow this link to one of my past blog posts where I describe this strategy in detail

11. **Monitor the Financial Health of Your Bank** - I recently posted on this topic; as bank failures are on the rise again, you need to watch the financial health of your bank carefully

12. **Live Within Your Means** - Make a household budget and live within it; make sure you don't spend more than you make - your largest monthly

cost is probably housing, is there anything you can do to reduce it? rent? buy? move? short sale? By the way, if you plan to short-sale your house, this year might be the time to do it as the debt forgiveness income will become taxable again after December 31, 2012 (unless Congress decides to extend it). Eating out and credit card charges are another place where you can easily cut household costs.

13. **Transportation** - Get rid of the old car that is costing you a lot of money to repair, especially if it is a gas guzzler, and buy a new, more fuel efficient car. Get a basic model without a lot of expensive, fancy features - a car is for transportation, after all. Pay cash if you can, but financing rates are pretty low if you have good credit. Gas prices have nowhere to go but up.

14. **Clear the Clutter** - Go through your house one room at a time and I'll bet you have a lot of new, unopened stuff (toys, household goods, gifts that were received or never given, etc.); sell it on EBay and get some cash for it! Your house will look a lot cleaner and you'll have some extra money that you can use to pay off credit cards or put in your emergency fund.

15. **Plant a Garden** - Homegrown food is organic, healthy and cheaper than buying from the store; it's also good to get outside and get some fresh air and exercise

16. **Insurance** - check your car insurance to see if you can get a better deal with another company; consider getting an umbrella liability policy to protect you from a lawsuit in excess of your auto or home coverage, especially if you have teenage drivers in the house or if you own rental property

17. **Read Motivational Books** - I like the Rich Dad, Poor Dad series myself, but there are lots of others; the best defense is a strong offense - look for investment and business opportunities when the markets are in turmoil and everyone is running for the hills

18. **Coffee** - I love my coffee; I also love my cheap drip coffeemaker, instead of the expensive Keurig with the K-cups - the K-cups cost a fortune compared to a bag of ground coffee; if you have to have Starbuck's, just get a cup of coffee and skip the fancy coffee drinks

19. **Charity** - Instead of giving cash to charity, donate lightly used items so you can get a tax deduction or better yet, volunteer your time to your favorite cause - it is much more valuable and you will feel better for it; if

you have kids do something that directly impacts them like working in the classroom or volunteering for their sports

20. **<u>Sense of Humor</u>** - No matter how tough things get, keep your sense of humor

Cartoosh's View

© 1-10-2009 Cartoosh.Com

Chapter 2 - Financial Fortress - Laying The Foundation

2012-09-15

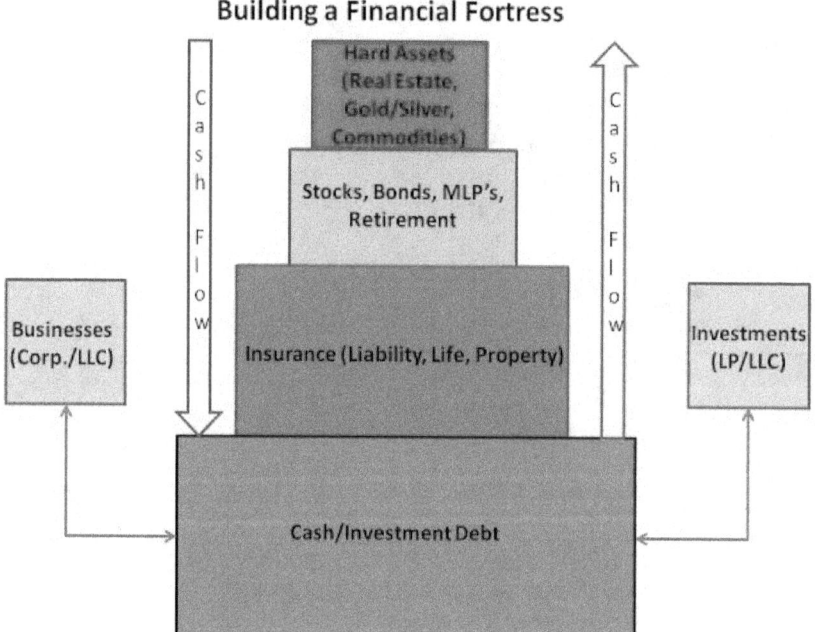

The foundation of your Financial Fortress is composed of two major components: <u>cash</u> and "good" debt. "Good" debt is <u>money</u> that you borrow for <u>investment</u> purposes. There are many sources of <u>good debt</u>, including a mortgage, <u>401(k)</u> loan, online sites such as <u>Prosper.com</u>, personal <u>bank loan</u>, friends/family, etc. If you have a great investment or <u>business idea</u> and put your mind to it, you can find a source of financing. "Bad" debt includes car loans,

Building A Financial Fortress

credit cards and personal loans that are taken out to buy clutter or things that don't put money back into your pocket either in the form of positive cash flow or a profit upon sale. Bad debt should be paid off as soon as possible. Why keep cash in a bank account that earns less than 1% when your car or credit card loan is many times higher than that? Cash is also critical for the foundation of your Financial Fortress. Your focus should be to increase your positive cash flow by using a budget, eliminating "bad debt" payments and carefully managing how much you spend. By saving money every month automatically (some call this "paying yourself first"), you can build your savings. Try to earn some yield on your cash, but be careful not to put too much in short term bond funds or money market accounts - they could lose value and if there is another financial crisis, you will be glad to have your FDIC insured accounts. There are opportunities to earn a higher yield without taking on too much risk.

By the way, if your company offers a 401(k) match, you should contribute enough to take full advantage of the match since that's really "free" money. I don't really like 401(k) investment options, but you can always roll over into a self-directed IRA when you take a new job and you'll have more options.

By using good debt, you don't need much of your own cash to make an investment. For example, you can buy an investment property worth $100,000 with $25,000 down and a bank will finance the rest. You control an asset worth 4x the amount you invested, which over time with inflation will grow in value. If properly managed, your property will maintain and grow its positive cash flow and you could enjoy reduced taxes from this kind of investment. The advantage of having positive cash flow is that you can withstand short-term fluctuations in value and continue to build the foundation of your Financial Fortress.

When investing, always think cash flow. It's often tempting to buy a stock that you think will go up in value so you can sell it, but that's market timing or speculation. Positive cash flow is always better because it adds to your foundation, allowing you to make additional investments.

Doom and Gloom - Inflation, Unemployment and the Dollar

2012-05-13

If you don't trust the stock market, think the bond market is primed for a crash and aren't sure if the real estate market has hit bottom yet, you are probably sitting on cash, suffering with paltry returns and waiting to see what to do next. Gold and silver may present a near-term buying opportunity due to their recent sell-off. Silver is especially intriguing since the performance spread between gold and silver has widened considerably since late in 2011 (see charts below).

Gold

I believe the long-term fundamentals continue to hold for precious metals

1-Year Historical Daily Closing Prices
Last price as of 20-Jun-2014: $20.87

Daily Closing Price — 100-Day M. A — 200-Day M. A

Silver

(higher inflation, weakening dollar and uncertainty in the global financial markets). Soon, the entire world will be printing money in an effort to avoid recession and austerity, which should be extremely bullish for the metals!

The very slow economic recovery in the United States faces many headwinds and could show signs of stalling out in the next couple of quarters. Indeed, there are already troubling signs such as weak employment numbers that are below expectations. The troubles in Europe, uncertainty about Asia/China economies, and structurally high unemployment and inflation in the United States will be difficult to overcome.

The actual rate of US inflation is likely much higher than what is being reported by official government statistics, which exclude food and energy components (significant costs for most people). The alternative measure keeps the methodology consistent from how it was done in 1980, which provides more of an "apples to apples" comparison of how inflation has trended over time. What is troubling about the chart below is that the disparity between the official statistics and the alternative measure has grown considerably since the early 90's.

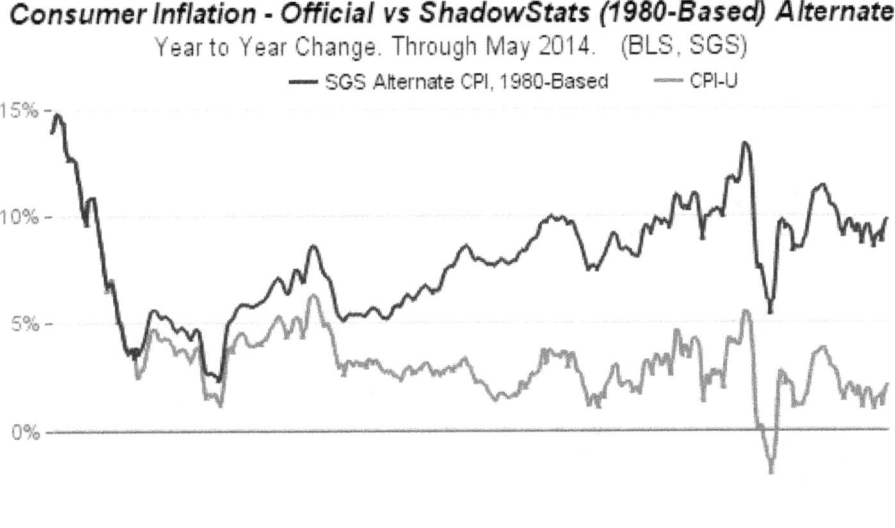

Consumer Inflation - Official vs ShadowStats (1980-Based) Alternate
Year to Year Change. Through May 2014. (BLS, SGS)
— SGS Alternate CPI, 1980-Based   — CPI-U

Published: June 17, 2014   shadowstats.com

The actual rate of unemployment is likely much higher than what is being reported as well, due to the large number of people who have given up trying to find a job (since these people are not considered "unemployed" in the official statistics). An estimate for these individuals is added back to the alternative measure to derive a more true measure of unemployment. As you can see, more than 1 in 5 people are estimated to be unemployed in the US and the number is **not** going down.

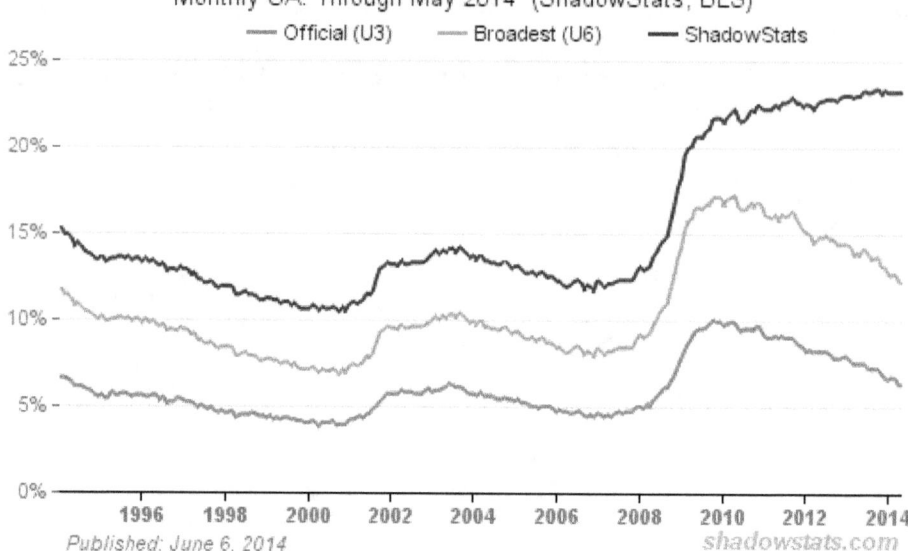

Unemployment Rate - Official (U-3 & U-6) vs ShadowStats Alternate
Monthly SA. Through May 2014 (ShadowStats, BLS)

— Official (U3) — Broadest (U6) — ShadowStats

Published: June 6, 2014

shadowstats.com

The dollar continues to be crushed by the Federal Reserve's continued effort to support the economy by printing money (low interest rates and quantitative easing). As you can see in the chart below, since the late 80's the dollar's purchasing power has declined by approximately 50% and there's no reason to see why this trend will not continue based on current Fed policy.

Financial- vs Trade-Weighted Dollar indices
Jan. 1985 Index = 100. Through Dec. 2013. (ShadowStats, FRB)

—— FRB Trade Weighted Dollar   —— ShadowStats Financial Weighted Dollar

Published: Dec. 31, 2013   shadowstats.com

It is important to have enough cash on hand for liquidity and emergencies - more is probably better given the economic uncertainties we now face. If you have excess cash available for investing, or if you have access to cheap borrowed funds at a low fixed rate, taking a position in gold or silver now might be a smart move.

Quote of the Day

2012-09-19

Be more concerned with your character than your reputation, because your character is what you really are, while your reputation is merely what others think you are – John Wooden.

Cash is (Still) King

2012-05-28

Reasons for being in cash right now:

A) Europe is on the verge of a financial meltdown that could dwarf the 2008 financial crisis - bank failures could lead to sovereign defaults - this will be felt globally
B) Bond yields are paltry and could get crushed if inflation picks up
C) Stock market has sold off but is still high relative to weak growth fundamentals
D) Real estate could take a header if there is another financial crisis, but will benefit from low interest rate environment in the meantime; price appreciation won't arrive until foreclosure inventory is gone - could be a few more years before that happens
E) Growth story (or lack of it) results in little direction for commodities

Longer term, real assets are better than financial assets if money printing by central banks continues (which seems like the most likely outcome to combat economic weakness and financial crisis).

Earn a Little More Interest

2011-04-02

If you are looking to earn a higher yield on your cash, here are a couple of ideas:

GE Interest Plus (not FDIC insured) currently offers up to 1.11% on short-term corporate notes.

American Express (FDIC insured) offers up to 0.9% on high yield savings accounts.

The More You Spend the More You Save

2012-09-01

How many times have you heard this? Well, if you buy two, you get the second for half off. Or, if you spend $100, we'll give you $5 off. It has gotten to where people actually believe that the more you spend the more you save. In reality, the more you spend, the more you spend. You aren't saving anything by buying more stuff. The best thing to do in these situations is just buy what you need right now and get the second (pick one - shirt, pair of shoes, bottle of shampoo, etc.) later when you really need it.

If you do have to make a purchase, make sure you use a coupon. I spend a lot of time in sporting goods stores with my kids and I'm usually able to Google a coupon on my phone and use it at the register if I don't have one in hand.

And a Few Thoughts on Car Maintenance:

You should always ask for a discount when you go to the car dealer for repairs (as I have several times recently to fix my 9 year old car). Because I have been back a few times, I ask for a discount -usually 10% and if I really whine they will give me 15%. If I didn't ask, I'd be paying 10% to 15% more. I'm sure they are still doing quite well (in fact, I know they are because they just moved into a new facility - flat screen TV's, K-cup coffee, a Subway and really nice furniture). I suppose I should try to use a cheaper mechanic, but when you work it's hard to get there and back when the dealer usually offers better hours and location.

I never buy tires from the car dealer or a tire shop. I have found that Costco is the best deal for tires (they usually have a coupon for $70 off a set of four tires - wait for those). You just can't be picky about the brand and you also need to go early in the day (before they open) or you won't get your tires. Costco also has great prices on batteries. I also like to buy gas from Costco since it's a lot cheaper than anywhere else - just have to wait in line.

FDIC Friday - 46 Failed Banks in 2012

2012-09-11

There have already been more <u>bank failures</u> in 2012 (46) than there were in 2008 (25), at the beginning of the <u>Great Recession</u>. This is certainly not a sign of a robust economy. If you bank with a small bank, keep an eye on it and make sure your deposits don't exceed the <u>FDIC insurance</u> limit ($250,000).

Building A Financial Fortress

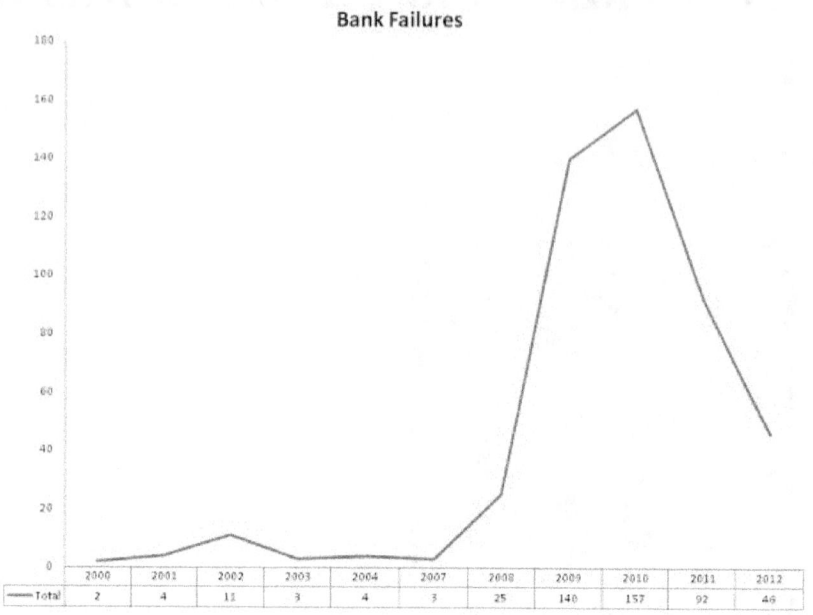

Bank Failures

	2000	2001	2002	2003	2004	2007	2008	2009	2010	2011	2012
Total	2	4	11	3	4	3	25	140	157	92	46

Tax Secrets of the Wealthy

2011-04-10

When I was living in Honolulu about 20 years ago, I remember a local TV show where this dude was talking about how the wealthy understand the tax code and are able to take advantage of the tax laws to increase their wealth. I never fully understood his message until very recently: **It doesn't matter how much you make, it's how much you keep**. His message still rings true today. If you work for a paycheck, most likely your only opportunity to reduce your taxes is with 401(k) or IRA contributions and a mortgage deduction. The net result is that you still pay a lot of taxes now and you will pay a lot of taxes in the future if your investments do well - your reward for being a good investor. Your house, I'm sorry to say, is not an investment - it's just a place to live.

The wealthy, on the other hand, have many strategies to reduce and defer taxes. They:

- Use a team of experts (i.e., attorney, accountant) to structure investments and their ownership to minimize taxes and liability, maximize returns and optimize estate planning
- Own one or more businesses, which allows for deduction of business expenses and payment of a salary to the owner (also a business expense)

Building A Financial Fortress

- Invest in tax-preferred investments such as municipal bonds and high dividend-yielding stocks
- Invest in oil/gas partnerships, which have various tax benefits including deferral of taxes on distributions, income tax credits and also hedge against inflation
- Own investment real estate, which provides positive cash flow and tax benefits due to depreciation and operating expense deductions that offset rental income, as well as a hedge against inflation
- Sell investment property using a 1031 exchange transaction, which allows for the deferral of taxes and the use of all of the sale proceeds to buy a new investment property
- Own real estate through limited liability entities and lease to their company(ies), which provides a tax deduction to the business (rent), minimizes taxable income at the entity owning the property due to depreciation and ownership expense deductions that offset the rental income, and allows for ultimate sale of the underlying business while retaining control over productive assets
- Invest in alternative investments (accredited investor)
- Use leverage (good debt) in investing in real estate and to create positive arbitrage - i.e., earning a higher after-tax rate of return than they are paying on the money
- Use life insurance to fund a portion of retirement needs and for estate planning

Obama care - Taxing Your Investment Income

2012-06-29

A little known fact about the Obama care legislation is that in order to cover the massive cost of the new legislation, there was a major expansion of taxes including adding a Medicare tax on net investment income for **everyone**, increased FICA taxes on "high income" taxpayers (individuals making more than $200K and couples making over $250K per year), limiting deductions for medical expenses and restricting the ability to use flexible spending accounts:

- Medicare tax on investment income (Sec. 1411): Imposes a tax on individuals equal to 3.8% of the lesser of the individual's net investment income for the year or the amount the individual's modified AGI exceeds a threshold amount. (Effective 2013.)

- **Additional hospital insurance tax on high-income taxpayers (Sec. 3101):** Employee portion of the Medicare hospital insurance tax part of FICA is increased by 0.9% on wages that exceed a threshold amount. (Effective 2013.)

- **Medical care itemized deduction threshold (Sec. 213):** Threshold for the itemized deduction for unreimbursed medical expenses is increased from 7.5% of adjusted gross income (AGI) to 10% of AGI for regular income tax purposes. (Effective 2013 generally, 2017 for certain taxpayers.)

- **Health flexible spending arrangements (FSAs) (Sec. 125(i)):** Maximum amount available for reimbursement of incurred medical expenses under a health FSA for a plan year (or other 12-month coverage period) must not exceed $2,500. (Effective 2013.)

- **Restrictions on use of HSA and FSA Funds (Sec. 223):** Amounts paid for over-the-counter medications will no longer be reimbursable from HSAs, Archer MSAs, health FSAs, or health reimbursement arrangements. (Effective 2011.)

The 3.8% Medicare tax on net investment income, which includes all types of investments including interest, dividends, capital gains, annuity income and rental income is perhaps the most concerning since it constitutes a significant broadening of the Medicare tax base. Previously, this type of tax would only be levied on earned (payroll) income and it affects everyone. This tax is a disincentive to investors, particularly those who own low-yielding "safe" investments such as money market funds, bonds or annuities. Sadly, even with the massive tax increase, the chances that the Obama care program will be "revenue neutral" are slim given the rate that healthcare costs are escalating in the US.

Medical care services, medical care, and all items
Annual average percent change in consumer price index

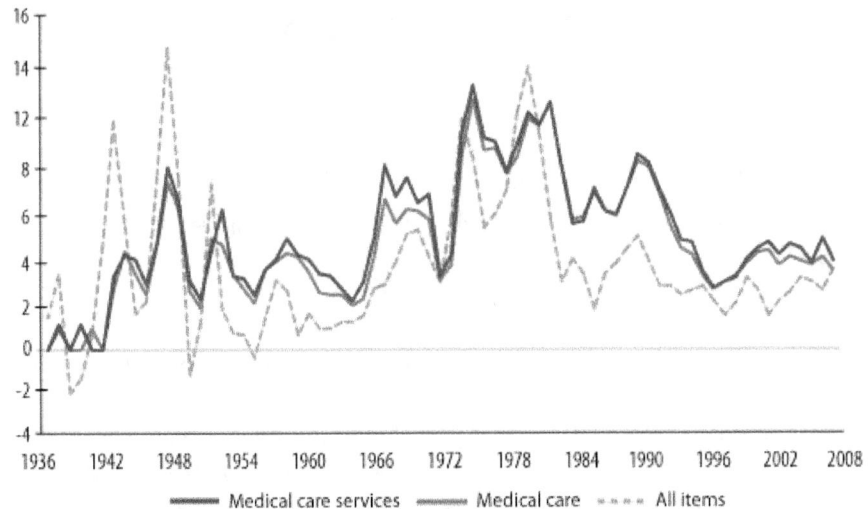

Source: U.S. Bureau of Labor Statistics

www.bls.gov

What Exactly is the "Fiscal Cliff" and Why Should I Care?

2012-07-20

The "Fiscal Cliff" you have been hearing about is the result of two major events that, if not delayed or otherwise modified by the US Congress, will occur in January 2013:

- US federal government spending cuts - these will happen automatically, the result of the 2011 debt ceiling deal
- Expiration of 2001-2003 tax cuts enacted during the Bush administration - in order to pass these tax cuts, Congress could not make them permanent (they had to expire in 10 years)

If nothing is done, the combination of the reduced government spending coupled with higher taxes will result in a drag on the economy that could be sufficient to put the economy back into recession (that is, if it isn't already in a recession). The Congressional Budget Office estimates the reduction in Gross Domestic Product (GDP) would be **4%!** A Wall St. Journal article from May 16, 2012 estimates the following impact in dollar terms: "In all, according to an analysis by J.P. Morgan economist Michael Feroli, $280 billion would be pulled out of the economy by the sun setting of the Bush tax cuts; $125 million from the expiration of the Obama payroll-tax holiday; $40 million from the expiration of emergency unemployment benefits; and $98 billion from Budget Control Act spending cuts. In all, the tax increases and spending cuts make up about 3.5% of GDP, with the Bush tax cuts making up about half of that, according to the J.P. Morgan report."

The Obama administration has said it is seeking tax increases for individuals who make more than $200,000/year and couples who make more than $250,000/year - i.e., the "rich." If you live on one of the coasts making that kind of money and have a few kids, a couple of cars and a mortgage, you are hardly rich.

Building A Financial Fortress

What is most likely to occur is that the Bush tax cuts will be temporarily extended and the spending cuts will be temporarily delayed - perhaps for a year or so, although current partisan political rhetoric is indicating "no deal" will be possible. The flip side of this, however, is that the US government debt continues to grow rapidly and will continue to grow until spending is curtailed and/or taxes are raised. By 2015, the gross public debt is projected to exceed $20 Trillion (already over $16 Trillion today)!

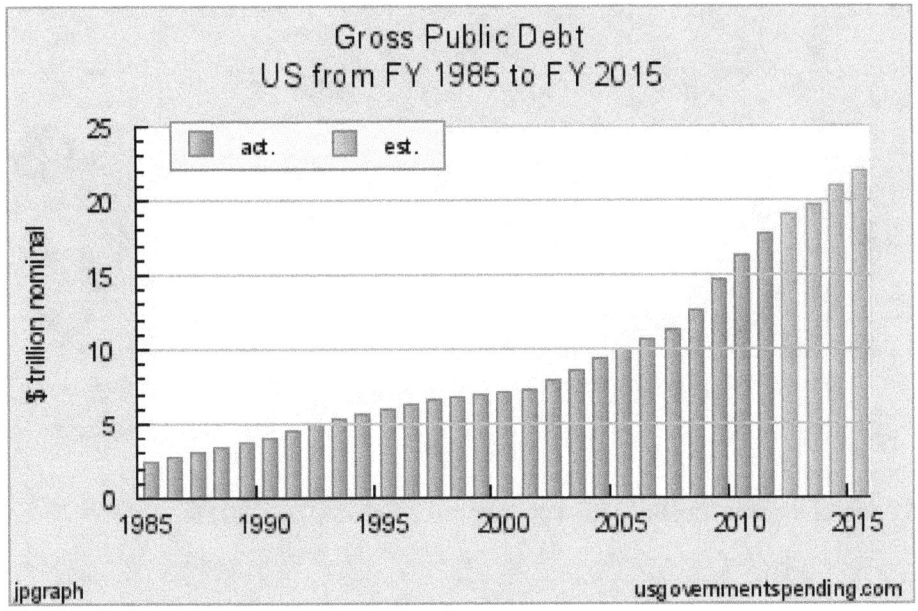

In the not too distant past, the top Federal tax rate was over 90%, as noted in the chart below. Do you think that eventually, taxes will return to those levels in order to service the growing mountain of government debt? This seems likely.

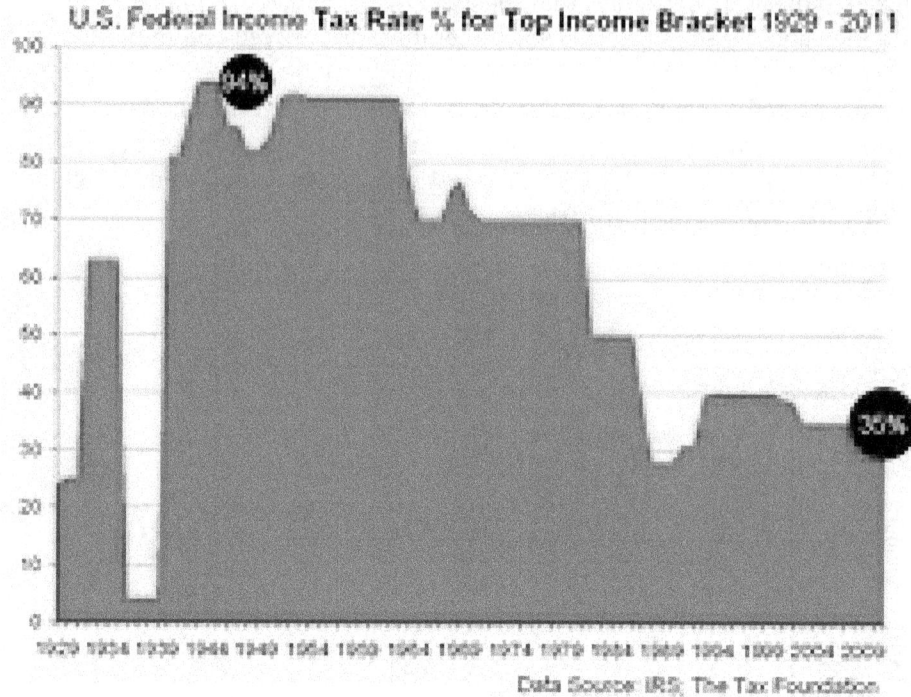

US Federal Income Tax Rate for Top Income Bracket 1929 - 2011

Protecting Your Wealth From Taxes

2012-11-10

It's now time to face the facts. Taxes are going up.

Printing money by <u>the Fed</u> and other central banks around the world is likely to continue for some time as a sneaky way to devalue the currency and reduce the debt burden. We see this reflected in the price of <u>gold</u> and <u>silver</u> lately and the long-term decline in the value of the dollar (chart below). This alone with not be enough, however, and taxes will need to be increased to deal with ballooning government deficits.

Financial- vs Trade-Weighted Dollar indices
Jan. 1985 Index = 100. Through Dec. 2013. (ShadowStats, FRB)

— FRB Trade Weighted Dollar   — ShadowStats Financial Weighted Dollar

Published: Dec. 31, 2013   shadowstats.com

Nationally, the fiscal cliff is approaching, and as seen in California (a state with a long history of anti-tax sentiment), voters will allow new taxes with the right amount of special interest advertising dollars backing it. In the case of Proposition 30, taxes are being raised on "wealthy" individuals and through the sales tax to fund schools. Sorry, but if you live on a coastal city like Los Angeles or New York and you have a few kids, a mortgage, a couple of car payments and make $250K+ a year (combined) that's just not wealthy. That's middle class. Maybe in Omaha, but not in LA.

Something I wasn't aware of is that **the income tax increase component of Proposition 30 is retroactive to the beginning of 2012!** Where that money actually goes is anyone's guess (they say it will be used for education, but how much of it gets to the classroom is questionable). Clearly, this is a disturbing precedent. California's revolt against taxes began in 1978 with Proposition 13, which limited the rate at which property taxes could be assessed and also limited the ability to increase taxes in the future by requiring a 2/3 majority vote of legislatures or the people (if a voter initiative). 34 years later, could we be at another turning point in how the majority of voters view taxes?

Building A Financial Fortress

Our national debt is now over $16 trillion and growing every day (check the link to the national debt clock). State budgets are bloated and state tax revenues are in decline from the after effects of the Great Recession and continued high unemployment (see chart below).

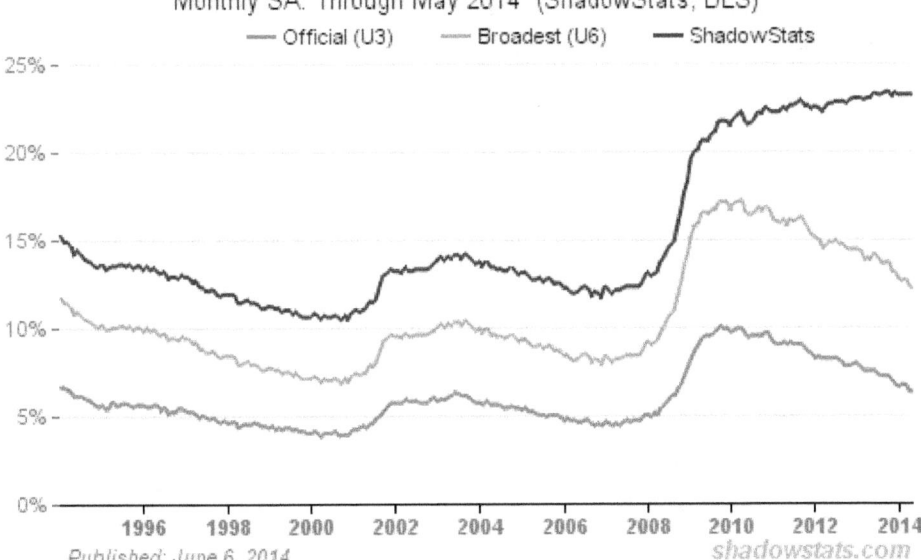

Unemployment Rate - Official (U-3 & U-6) vs ShadowStats Alternate
Monthly SA. Through May 2014 (ShadowStats, BLS)

— Official (U3)　　— Broadest (U6)　　— ShadowStats

Published: June 6, 2014　　shadowstats.com

With Obama care, taxes have already increased; including a major expansion of the Medicare tax to include net investment income (see my past blog post on this topic for more information). With Obama winning four more years, it seems likely that this trend will continue at the national level.

Clearly, if you work for a salary you will pay the price in higher taxes. Now more than ever it will be critical to make tax planning an important part of your investment and retirement planning.

Important investment tools available for anyone to use in tax planning include:

- Federal (and state in some cases) tax free municipal bonds, including land secured bonds
- Oil and gas master limited partnerships

Building A Financial Fortress

- Life insurance as a retirement vehicle
- Precious metals (to protect against the decline of the dollar)
- Roth IRA
- Investment real property (think of it as a long term inflation protected bond - as long as the cash flow is positive)

Don't wait until it's too late. Start your tax planning now - talk to a CPA or tax preparer who is knowledgeable about your particular situation.

Taxes

2014-03-02

Tax Day - April 15 is coming up fast. I have used TurboTax for many years and have gotten to where I don't need to do the interview and I can just directly enter the information. A lot has changed since I first started using it - you can upload just about anything now, from your paycheck information, 1099's from investments, etc. without having to retype everything, which is really nice. I have also gotten to like the electronic filing and automatic deposit of refunds. I don't even print my tax return anymore - just save a pdf file on a disc and file it with the backup paperwork. It's always a little nerve-racking preparing the tax return because I'm never totally sure exactly what the refund or tax due will be. So many things can happen during a year and estimating the tax impact, especially if you have stock sales or other types of taxable transactions like sales of real property or other capital assets, can be challenging, even for a CPA. This is especially difficult if you are paid a salary and rely totally on tax withholding to cover your annual tax bill. This year was made more difficult by the new Obama care taxes on investment income and higher Alternative Minimum Tax. Also, differences in the state taxation of Healthcare Spending Account contributions were a bit of a surprise to me. One thing that is clear is that taxes continue to rise and tax planning really needs to be a year-round process - not just something you do in December.

Quandary

2011-05-29

These are trying times. Being in cash is safe and feels good, but with the dollar's value slowly disappearing on a daily basis and virtually zero interest rates on savings, not a great place to be for too long.

Financial- vs Trade-Weighted Dollar indices
Jan. 1985 Index = 100. Through Dec. 2013. (ShadowStats, FRB)

— FRB Trade Weighted Dollar   — ShadowStats Financial Weighted Dollar

Published: Dec. 31, 2013   shadowstats.com

Many other investment opportunities are looking a bit overbought, including stocks and commodities, which have enjoyed a strong run-up over the past couple of years. Bonds (especially US Treasury securities) are concerning, given signs of inflation brewing and historically low yields. Where, then, to invest?
 For now, the best course of action may be to do nothing until we have a better idea of where unemployment, housing and the economy in general are headed. While things aren't as bad as they were three years ago, they aren't that great either. Unemployment is stubbornly high. Housing, which typically leads the economy out of recession, is still very weak. The overall economy is barely showing growth. Some are even calling a "double dip" recession now.

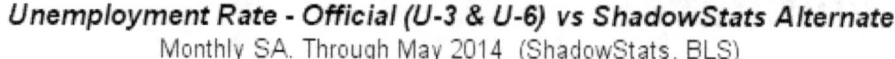

Unemployment Rate - Official (U-3 & U-6) vs ShadowStats Alternate
Monthly SA. Through May 2014 (ShadowStats, BLS)

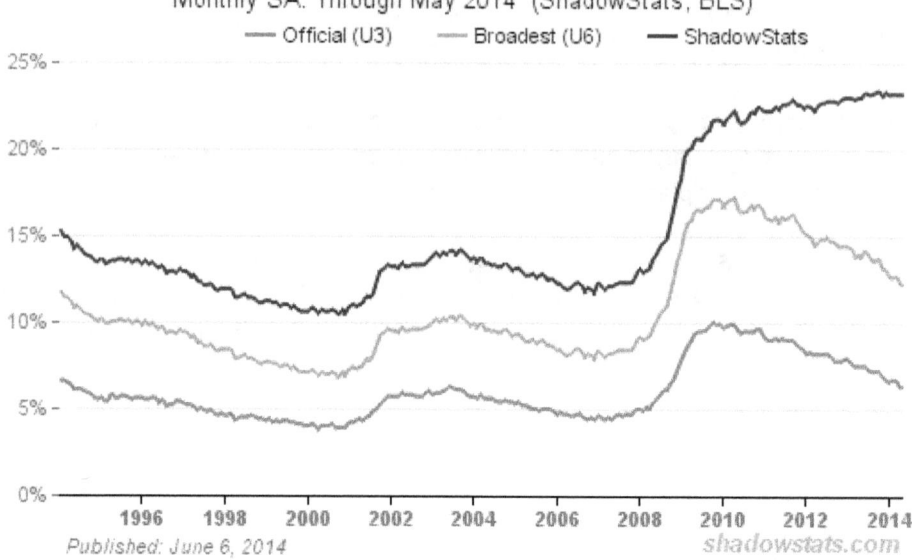

Published: June 6, 2014   shadowstats.com

In the meantime, I really like the oil & gas master limited partnerships, where you can get a 7 - 8 percent yield with commodity upside (energy will always be in demand and over time, this is a great long term investment). You also get tax deferral on most of the cash distributions you receive. Plan to buy and hold these investments. If you sell, you have to pay ordinary income taxes on the portion of the distributions that were not previously taxed in addition to the capital gains taxes you normally pay when selling any stock - a major bummer at tax time. Also, the work required to incorporate these into your tax return is substantial, so be prepared. Most of the major banks/investment companies have sector reports on master limited partnerships that are good to read for an overview of the industry and to help you select a few to invest in.

Chapter 3 - Building a Financial Fortress - The Next Level - Insurance

2012-09-21

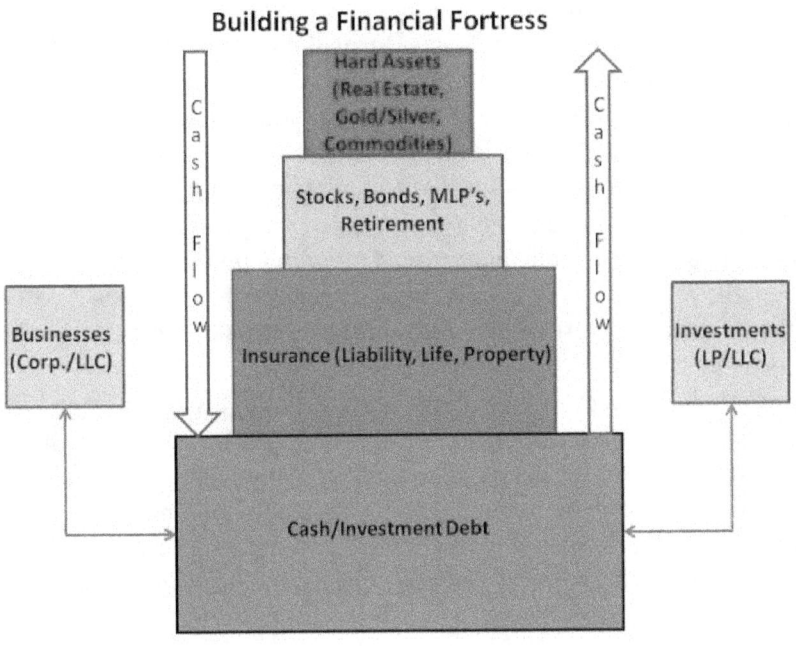

ntaining an adequate amount of insurance is essential to build a strong Financial Fortress. Insurance provides a buffer against uncertainties to protect your wealth and in the case of life insurance can also provide a retirement planning option.

Insurance comes in three main categories:

1. **Liability** - this can include a portion of the insurance you have on your car, a personal or business "umbrella" liability policy that provides excess coverage, or liability coverage maintained on an investment property; liability insurance is very important to have if someone is injured in a car accident or at one of your investment properties - as a general rule, you should maintain liability coverage at least equal to your net worth (home equity plus all other assets, minus liabilities); umbrella policies are relatively cheap and are a good source of excess liability coverage - if you have significant net worth, you can't afford not to have one

2. **Life** - there are many different types of life insurance, but the two main types are term life and whole life - term life buys you insurance for a period of time although the rate you pay typically goes up as you get older, whole life is "permanent" as long as you continue to pay the premiums and is usually a level payment; the nice thing about a whole life policy is that it grows in value annually (the "cash surrender value") and you can borrow against it to fund your retirement - loans are not income, are not taxable and are paid off with a portion of the death benefit; you really only need a small amount of life insurance if you are single, but once married and with kids you'll need to increase your coverage

3. **Property** - protects your property in the event of loss or damage (fire, theft, etc.) - most common is your homeowner's policy but can also include insurance for personal articles (i.e., wedding ring), rental property and a portion of your car insurance policy; for a homeowner's or rental property policy, it's a good idea to make sure the coverage includes replacement cost and code upgrades - check annually at renewal time

It may also be beneficial to buy all your insurance from one of the larger insurance companies since they offer discounts on multiple policies.

Life Insurance - A Good Retirement Planning Alternative

2011-03-28

One of the drawbacks of traditional retirement accounts such as IRA's and 401(k)'s is the fact that they require minimum distributions, whether you need the money or not, after age 70 1/2. In addition, the withdrawals are taxed as ordinary income at the tax rates in effect at the time. Your reward for being an excellent investor is to pay much of what you make in investment earnings back to the government in taxes. It seems unlikely that tax rates will be lower in the future than they are today with all of the borrowing our government is doing, so the notion that somehow you will be in a lower tax bracket in retirement doesn't make as much sense anymore.

An interesting alternative retirement plan idea is to buy a life insurance policy with a very low death benefit. You then pay the maximum premium allowable under IRS guidelines, without the policy becoming a Modified Endowment

Building A Financial Fortress

Contract or "MEC," where distributions including policy loans become taxable and potentially subject to penalties. The cash surrender value of the policy grows tax free. Funds can then be withdrawn in retirement by taking out loans against the policy (loans are not taxable). The loans would then be repaid out of the death benefit, with any excess paid to the beneficiaries of the policy.

A great book on this subject is Missed Fortune 101: A Starter Kit to Becoming a Millionaire, by Douglas R. Andrew. You must be willing to commit some time to understanding life insurance, which can be challenging. You will also need to consult with your tax advisor to make sure there are no issues in your specific situation. You may cringe when the author suggests that you borrow out your home equity as a source of funding for the up-front life insurance premium payments. At the same time, the concept that home equity is neither liquid nor safe is not lost on most of us having survived the Great Recession.

One of the biggest advantages to the life insurance retirement plan is that you are not required to take minimum distributions with an insurance policy and as mentioned previously, policy loans are not taxable as long as the policy is not a "MEC." You have to have confidence in the investment prowess and business savvy of the insurance company you choose to issue the policy. The good news is that insurance companies fare pretty well - just look at how many banks failed in the current downturn versus insurance companies. Also, insurance companies tend to be fairly conservative in their overall investment portfolios.

Chapter 4 - Financial Fortress – Stocks, Bonds, MLP's

2012-09-29

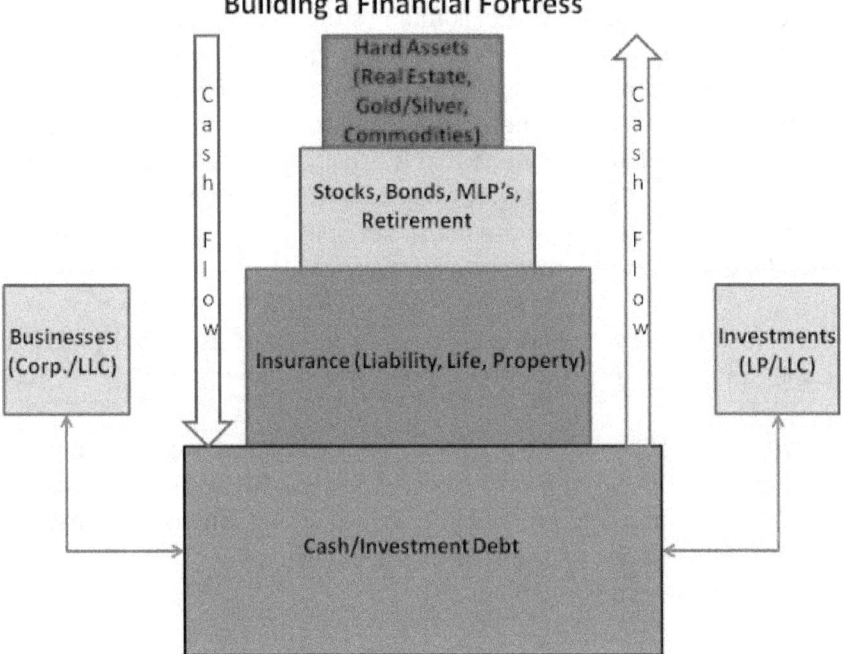

Once you have adequate cash to invest and insurance coverage, the next level in the Financial Fortress is investing in some paper assets. These include stocks, bonds, shares in Master Limited Partnerships and retirement accounts.

I will cover each one in a separate post.

Building A Financial Fortress

Stocks

In my view, it's much better to own 100% of a business, such as a small company that manufactures and/or sells products, a consultancy or a real estate property investment and management business. This is because you have total control over all the business decisions, the risks that are taken and you also enjoy all of the profits (and unfortunately also suffer all of the losses). Sometimes, however, owning less than 100% of a company can be a nice way to participate in a great business without having to spend the time managing or making huge cash investment. Even better if that ownership interest can be bought and sold instantly in a highly liquid stock market.

There are two main types of stock: common stock and preferred stock. In many ways, preferred stock is a lot like debt - it has a liquidation preference, which means that in the event the company goes bankrupt, preferred shareholders receive their money before common shareholders. Also, preferred stock typically pays a mandatory dividend that is usually higher than the common stock dividend. Preferred stock may also be convertible into common stock (similar to some types of corporate debt), but unlike common stock does not allow the holder to vote on corporate matters.

Common stock shares in the profits and losses of a company, usually has voting rights and can also receive a dividend, if declared by the company.

I'm not a huge fan of buying stock mutual funds with taxable money or self-directed IRA's. You may not have a choice with your 401(k) but you do with your taxable funds and self-directed IRA. Why pay someone who probably isn't any smarter than you are to pick stocks? They make money on their management fee whether you do or not.

Instead, pick a few companies in industries you know or understand and wait for the stock price to reach an attractive value to purchase. I'll never forget a story about a stock broker who recommended buying Lowe's just prior to the Great Recession, when the individual really wanted to buy Costco, being a regular shopper there and seeing firsthand what a terrific company it is from the perspective of a customer. She relented to the broker and ended up being very unhappy with the Lowe's investment since it performed very poorly as people stopped doing home improvement work as the value of their homes plummeted, while Costco did especially well during the recession with shoppers gravitating toward low prices and value.

Similarly, who would have thought that throughout the Great Recession, people would have to have their latte's and techno-gadgets (simple pleasures?), which allowed Apple and Starbucks to prosper during the worst downturn since the Great Depression? Stock brokers have also at various times recommended selling shares of Apple in order to be more "diversified." If you own a few companies and don't have all your wealth in stocks, you don't need that kind of diversification. If you sold Apple, what would you do with the money anyway, besides pay taxes?

Here are a few other thoughts on diversification:

Warren Buffett says, "Diversification is protection against ignorance."
Peter Lynch has referred to diversification as "deworsification," especially when it came to companies diversifying into non-core businesses.

Charlie Munger says "Wide diversification, which necessarily includes investment in mediocre businesses, only guarantees ordinary results."

Bottom line: take the time to do the research and make your own decisions. Pick a few good companies and stick with them. I also don't recommend a large percentage of your assets in stocks. If the stock market suffers a 50%+ loss, you don't want to have the same thing happen to your investment portfolio. Stocks that pay a dividend are great, but be careful because the dividend can always be cut. The dividend yield may look attractive, but it may be short-lived.

Quote of the Day - David Lee Roth on Wealth

2012-09-07

"Money can't buy happiness but it can buy a huge yacht that sails right next to it."
— David Lee Roth

Who Cares About the Stock Market Anyway?

2011-06-11

My philosophy for the past few years has been to focus on investing for positive cash flow. By investing for positive cash flow, you can free yourself from the worries of whether your asset has gone up or down in value in the short term - if you have purchased a good asset at the right price (investment real estate, oil/gas limited partnership interest, dividend-paying stock, high yield note, etc.) that pays you cash on a regular basis, short term value fluctuations will not matter.

So what is going on with the stock market lately? If you look at the chart below, the stock market (using the Dow Jones Industrial Average) has benefited greatly over the past year by a more or less steady decline in the value of the dollar (DXY). The decline in the dollar is largely the result of Federal Reserve policy to keep interest rates low, including the quantitative easing. Recently, the dollar has strengthened in response to continued turmoil in Europe. As you can see, dollar strength/weakness is inversely correlated with the stock market and slight movements in the dollar index translate into significant movements in the stock market. Further downside risk to the stock market (and commodities markets, which are all priced in dollars, such as gold and oil) exists in the short term as long as the dollar continues to strengthen.

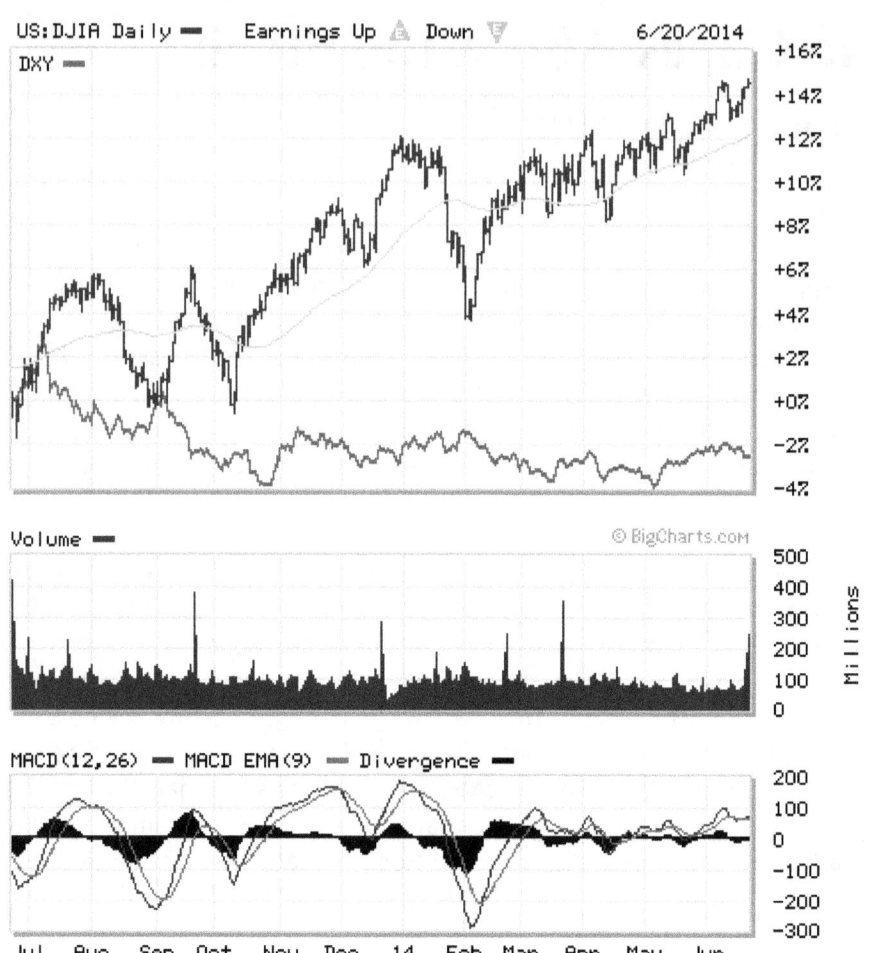

How long can global demand keep up with the continuous supply of dollars being printed every day? Only time will tell. As you can see in the chart below, the money supply has been growing again since early last year after peaking in 2008.

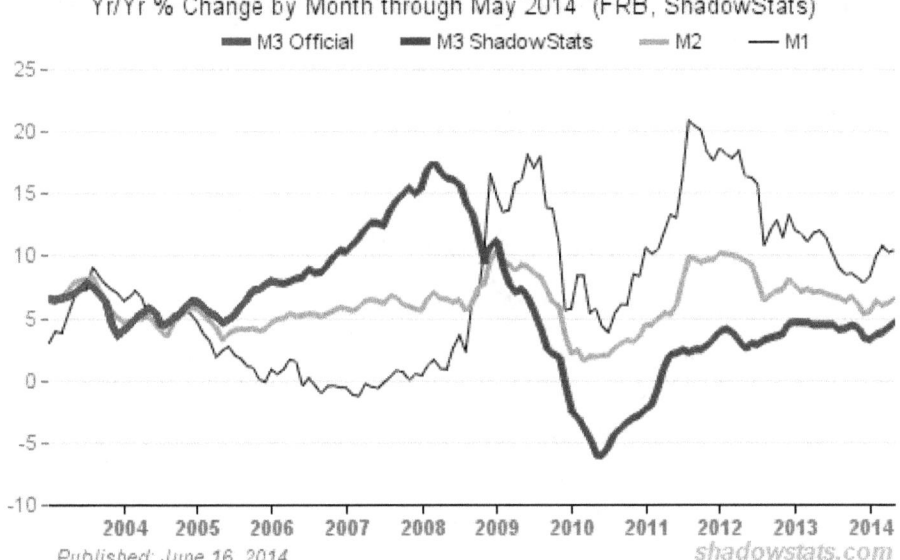

Annual U.S. Money Supply Growth - ShadowStats Continuation
Yr/Yr % Change by Month through May 2014 (FRB, ShadowStats)

Published: June 16, 2014

shadowstats.com

One thing is for sure; inflation will continue to hurt savers and will benefit those who borrow at fixed rates for the foreseeable future. Official government statistics for inflation (CPI) understate the real rate of inflation (see chart below).

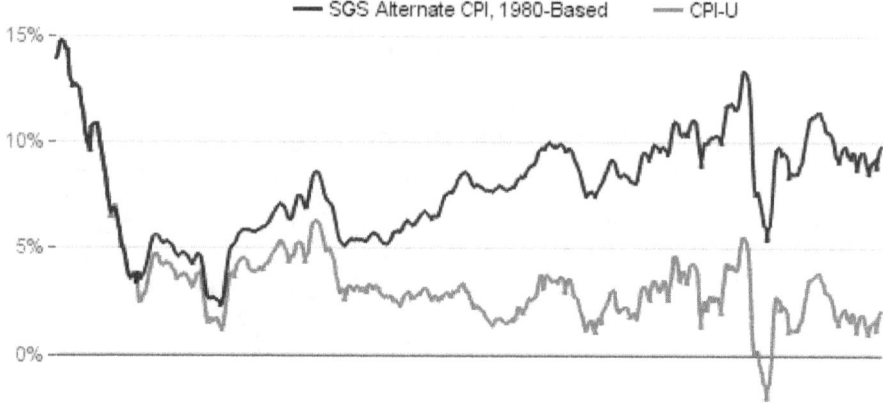

Consumer Inflation - Official vs ShadowStats (1980-Based) Alternate
Year to Year Change. Through May 2014.   (BLS, SGS)

— SGS Alternate CPI, 1980-Based   — CPI-U

Published: June 17, 2014   shadowstats.com

Stock Market and Dollar Rally? What's Wrong With This Picture?

2012-08-06

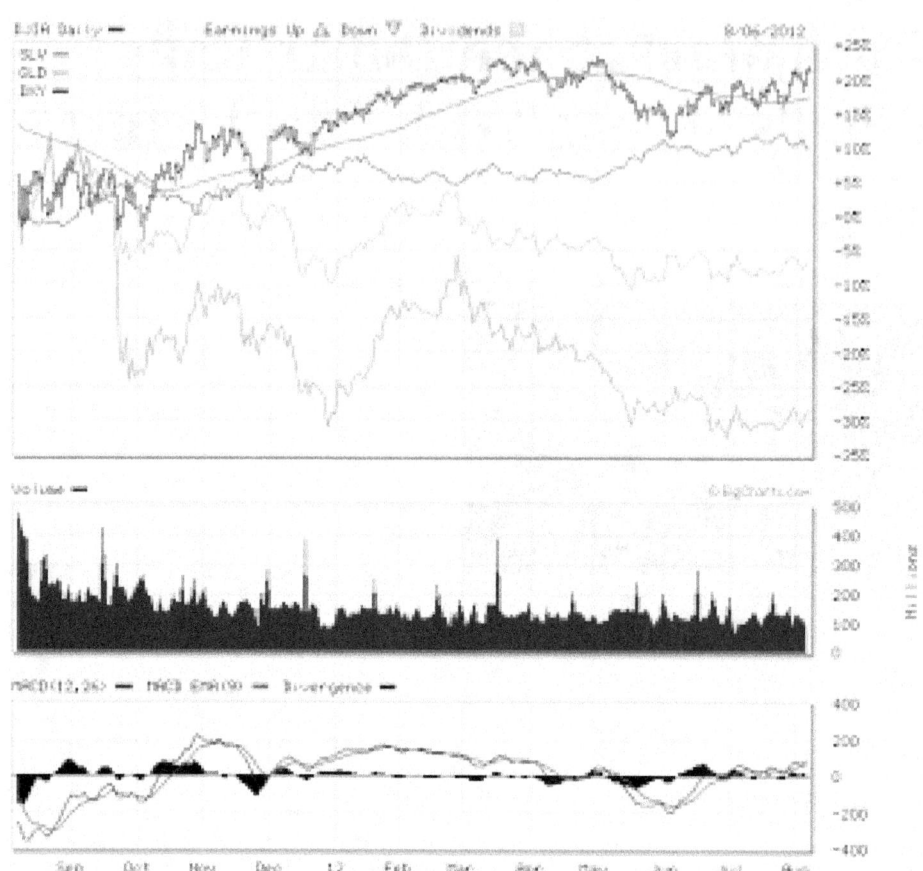

As you can see in the chart, silver (SLV) is down 30% over the past year and gold (GLD) is down 5% while the dollar (DXY) is up 10% and the stock market (DJIA) is up over 20%.

This looks like an opportunity to buy silver and gold and/or sell or short the stock market and the dollar. The stock market increase over the past year certainly isn't because the US economy is doing great (8.3% official rate of unemployment, 1.5% growth in GDP, etc.). Also, with the Federal Reserve's "easy money" policy, the dollar's recent appreciation is sure to be short-lived, and the dollar seems almost certain to continue declining in value - possibly at an accelerated pace, just as it has for years (see chart below):

Building A Financial Fortress

Financial- vs Trade-Weighted Dollar indices
Jan. 1985 Index = 100. Through Dec. 2013. (ShadowStats, FRB)

— FRB Trade Weighted Dollar — ShadowStats Financial Weighted Dollar

Published: Dec. 31, 2013

shadowstats.com

Speculators seem to have moved from gold and silver into the dollar and the stock market, fueled by cheap credit. Also driving the dollar (and Treasuries, which continue to have very low yields) is the periodic fear/panic that accompanies the Europe story, when investors rush into Treasuries for "safety."

Funds have continued to flow into bond mutual funds and out of stock mutual funds as individual investors continue to prefer safety and yield over capital gains (or losses), which means that the stock market rally is being led by Wall Street "smart money." But even the "smart money" makes dumb moves, like JP Morgan's $5.8 billion trading loss or more recently, the "Knightmare" on Wall Street. Treasury yields have dropped almost 1% over the past year due to continued strong demand. Recently, there is more investor interest in municipal bonds as well as corporate bonds in addition to Treasuries.

Here are some interesting ways to short the dollar:

- UDN -

The investment seeks to track the price and yield performance, before fees and expenses, of the Deutsche Bank Short US Dollar Futures Index. The index is comprised solely of short futures contracts. The futures contract is designed to replicate the performance of being short the US Dollar against the Euro, Japanese Yen, British Pound, Canadian Dollar, Swedish Krona and Swiss Franc.

- CYB -

The investment seeks to achieve total returns reflective of both money market rates in China available to foreign investors and changes in value of the Chinese Yuan relative to the U.S. dollar. The fund normally invests at least 80% of its net assets, plus the amount of any borrowings for investment purposes, in investments whose combined performance is economically tied to China. It is an actively managed exchange traded fund that seeks to achieve its investment objective by investing in short-term securities and instruments designed to provide exposure to Chinese currency and money market rates. The fund is non-diversified.

I have written previously about the strategy of going long on the Chinese currency as a short play against the dollar.

Here are some interesting ways to short the stock market:

- HDGE The investment seeks capital appreciation through short sales of domestically traded equity securities. The fund seeks to achieve the fund'™s investment objective by short selling a portfolio of liquid mid- and large-cap U.S. exchange-traded equity securities, ETFs registered pursuant to the Investment Company Act of 1940, ETNs and other ETPs. On a day-to-day basis, it may hold U.S. government securities, short-term high quality fixed income securities, money market instruments, overnight and fixed-term repurchase agreements, cash and cash equivalents with maturities of one year or less for investment purposes and to cover its short positions.

- Other ETF's

If you want to invest in silver or gold, I recommend physical coins (store in a safe or bank safe deposit box for security) - preferably US Silver Eagle or Gold Buffalo bullion coins. These are available from reputable coin dealers - you can easily check the prices on EBay.

Searching for High Dividend Yields? Don't Expect Safety.

2012-08-13

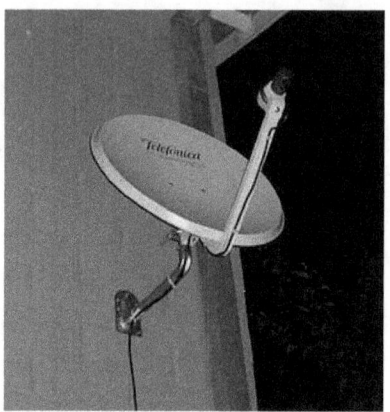

If you are looking for high dividend yields, take a look at the following stocks, all of which have a large market capitalization (over $5 billion) and solid return on equity. A couple of these have been hit hard by the recession in Europe:

1) Telefonica SA (TEF) - dividend yield was 12.1%; return on equity for the last 12 months is 28.3% and market capitalization is $55 billion; you'll have to wait until they reinstate the dividend, since it was recently suspended so they could pay down some of their debt - dividend could return in 2013

- Telefonica, S.A. is a telecommunications group which provides a range of services through its telecommunications networks mainly focused on providing fixed and mobile telephony services and present mainly in Spain, Europe and Latin America.

2) France Telecom (FTE) - current dividend yield is 10.9%; return on equity for the last 12 months is 14.2% and market capitalization is $36 billion; there are rumors that the dividend will be reduced in 2013

- France Telecom SA provides telecommunications services to residential, professional, and large business customers. Company offers public fixed-line telephone, leased lines and data transmission, mobile telecommunications, cable television, Internet etc.

3) Energy Transfer Partners (ETP) - current dividend yield is 8%; return on equity for the last 12 months is 13.6% and market capitalization is $6.9 billion

- Energy Transfer Partners, L.P. is a publicly traded partnership owning and operating a portfolio of energy assets (pipeline transportation of natural gas).

I really liked AT&T (T) when the dividend yield was over 6% a year ago. Now it is 4.7%.

Bottom line is if you go chasing dividend yield, be cautious since a high yield may not last for very long.

Omeros Looks Like a Good Biotech Play

2012-09-02

Disclosure: My family and I own positions in Omeros.

I don't normally like to talk about individual stocks, but occasionally I do like to invest in companies that either represent a great value or present an excellent opportunity for growth.

Omeros Corp (OMER) is a clinical stage biopharmaceutical company that engages in discovering, developing and commercializing products targeting inflammation, coagulopathies and disorders of the central nervous system. The company's products are derived from its proprietary PharmacoSurgery platform designed to improve clinical outcomes of patients undergoing arthroscopic, ophthalmological, urological and other surgical and medical procedures. It also has a deep and diverse pipeline of preclinical programs as well as a platform capable of unlocking new drug targets. The company was founded by Gregory A. Demopulos and Pamela Pierce Palmer on June 16, 1994 and is headquartered in Seattle, WA.

I was a little unhappy that they recently did a secondary offering at $10 when the stock was trading at $13, which resulted in a big one day decline in the stock price, but they do need to continue to fund their development pipeline, which is very interesting as you'll see below. Over the past four quarters through June 30, 2012, they had a cash "burn rate" of ($26) million. If you use the most recent (June 30, 2012) quarter's cash burn rate of ($9) million, Omeros has a ($36) million annualized cash burn rate. After the recent stock sale (which netted proceeds of $32 million plus cash on hand of slightly more than $7 million), the Company will have approximately $40 million in cash. This should support it for the next twelve months, assuming the annualized burn rate of $36 million. This will need be confirmed by a "clean" audit report in their December 31, 2012 annual report.

Building A Financial Fortress

The Company is currently in late stages of development of two drugs that reduce inflammation and promote recovery during and after eye and knee surgery. The Company recently announced a successful initial Phase 3 trial for one compound (OMS 302), the eye surgery candidate. OMS 302 and another compound (OMS 103HP, the knee surgery candidate) are in Phase 3 trials.

Below is a quick summary of how clinical trials for new drugs work:

The Research Phases

Before a drug can be approved for sale to the public there is a set of clinical tests that must be performed. There is the Pre-Clinical Research Stage. Here the drug is synthesized and purified. Animal tests are performed, and institutional review boards assess the studies and make recommendations on how to proceed. If the recommendations are positive, then an application to the FDA occurs and clinical tests begin.

Phase 1: clinical studies in this phase represent the first time that an IND is tested on humans either healthy volunteers or sometimes patients. The purpose of these studies is study in a clinical setting the metabolism, structure-reactivity relationships, mechanism olfaction, and side effects of the drug in humans. If possible, phase 1 studies are used to determine how effective the drug is. Phase 1 studies are usually conducted on 20 to 80 subjects.

The purpose of phase 2 clinical trials is to determine the efficacy of a drug to treat patients with a specific disease or condition, as well as learn about common short-term side effects or risks. These studies are conducted on a larger scale than phase 1 studies and typically involve several hundred patients.

Phase 3 clinical trials provide more information about the effects and safety of the drug and they allow scientists to extrapolate the results of clinical studies to the general population. Phase 3 studies generally involve several hundred to several thousand people.

Completion of Phase 3 trials means that the Company can request New Drug Application approval from the Federal Drug Administration. If approved, the Company will be able to market the drug and generate revenue, either by making and selling the drug itself or licensing it out. It can take 8+ years to develop a new drug through the entire clinical development process through approval, so you have to be patient (no pun intended) and have adequate capital to fund the development effort.

Promising Experimental Drugs

Eight years is a long time to review a drug. Some patients, especially terminally ill patients, don't particularly care if the drug meets high standards of safety. They don't have the time. Taking any drug, in their view, is better than the alternative. So today's policies also allow some investigational drugs even before they are approved for marketing.

These new policies called "expanded access" protocols include the Treatment Investigational New Drug (IND) application and the parallel track mechanism. Both tracks allow promising drugs, not yet approved for marketing, to be used in moderately unrestricted studies where the intent is not only to learn more about the drug, especially about its safety, but also to provide treatment for people with no real alternative. But these expanded access protocols still require clinical researchers to formally investigate the drug in well-controlled studies and to supply some evidence that the drug is likely to be helpful.

Below is a graphic showing Omeros' current product pipeline (note that four drug candidates are planned for the IND application described above):

Product Pipeline

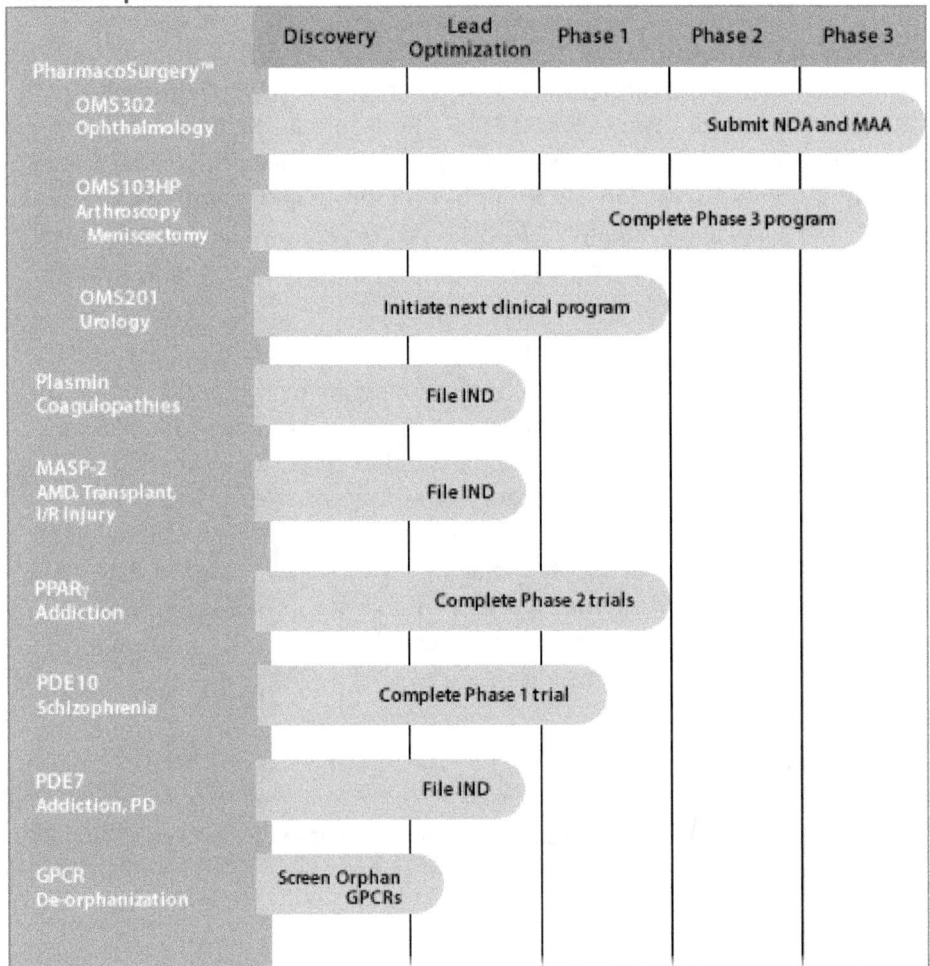

Of greatest interest is the Company's program for unlocking "orphan receptors," the last but certainly not least item on the pipeline above. Orphan receptors are very valuable for drug development, as the Company describes below: "GPCRs, which mediate key physiological processes in the body, are one of the most valuable families of drug targets. According to Insight Pharma Reports, GPCR-targeting drugs represent 30 to 40 percent of marketed pharmaceuticals. Examples include Claritin® (allergy), Zantac® (ulcers and reflux), OxyContin® (pain), Lopressor® (high blood pressure), Imitrex® (migraine headache), Reglan®

(nausea) and Abilify® (schizophrenia, bipolar disease and depression) as well as all other antihistamines, opioids, alpha and beta blockers, serotonergics and dopaminergics.

The industry focuses its GPCR drug discovery efforts mostly on non-sensory GPCRs. Of the 363 total non-sensory GPCRs, approximately 240 have known ligands (molecules that bind the receptors) with nearly half of those targeted either by marketed drugs (46 GPCRs) or by drugs in development (about 70 GPCRs). There are approximately 120 GPCRs with no known ligands, which are termed "orphan GPCRs." Without a known ligand, drug development for a given receptor is extremely difficult.

Omeros uses its proprietary high-throughput CRA to identify small-molecule agonists and antagonists for orphan GPCRs, unlocking them to drug development. **Omeros** believes that it is the first to possess the capability to unlock orphan GPCRs in high-throughput, and that currently there is no other comparable technology. Unlocking these receptors could lead to the development of drugs that act at these new targets. There is a broad range of indications linked to orphan GPCRs including cardiovascular disease, asthma, diabetes, pain, obesity, Alzheimer's disease, Parkinson's disease, multiple sclerosis, schizophrenia, learning and cognitive disorders, autism, osteoporosis, osteoarthritis and several forms of cancer."

Biotech stocks are certainly very risky investments and this one is no exception. However, Omeros has a deep product pipeline for an 8 year old company. They also have a good strategy and execution so far and some of the drug candidates could be game changers (i.e., Addiction, Schizophrenia).

Stock Market Crash Ahead?
Should You Care?

2012-10-19

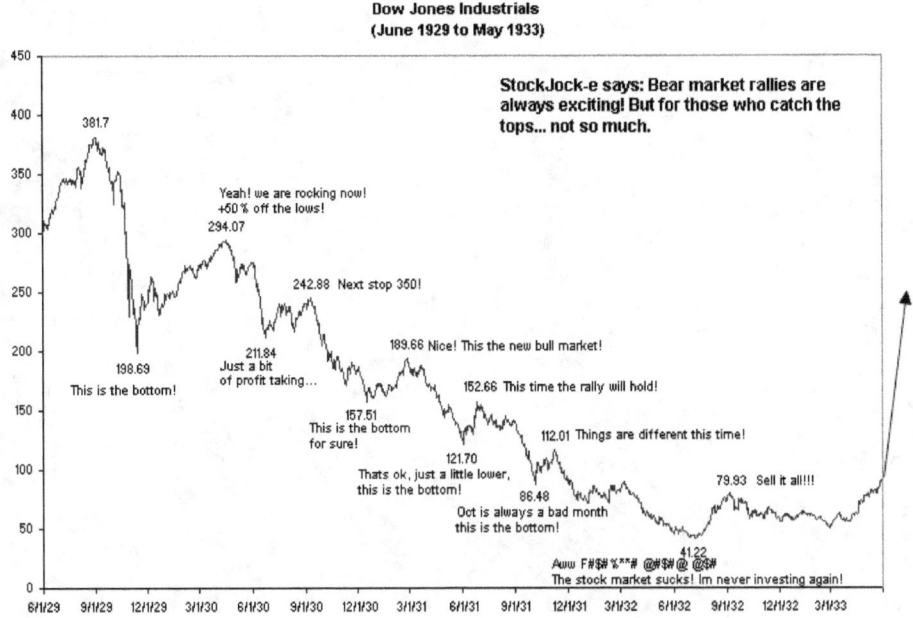

Dow Jones Industrials
(June 1929 to May 1933)

StockJock-e says: Bear market rallies are always exciting! But for those who catch the tops... not so much.

The chart above says it all - everyone is always hopeful that the stock market has found a bottom after a sell-off. After the crash of 1929, it took almost four years for the market to finally find a bottom. If you look at the chart below showing the last five years (beginning with the sell-off in 2008), the bottom seemed to arrive quickly and then the money printing started. One could argue that the market hasn't really found a bottom yet from the most recent downturn and today's 205 point loss could just be the beginning of another significant downturn (as some are now predicting).

I don't advocate having more than a 20% exposure to the stock market at any time. While you may miss out on good times, in bad times and periods of significant volatility, you won't risk being completely wiped out by a stock market crash. If you follow the principles of the Financial Fortress, your focus will be where it should be - cash flow, proper diversification and risk management.

Stock Market Outlook - Short Term/Long Term

2012-11-23

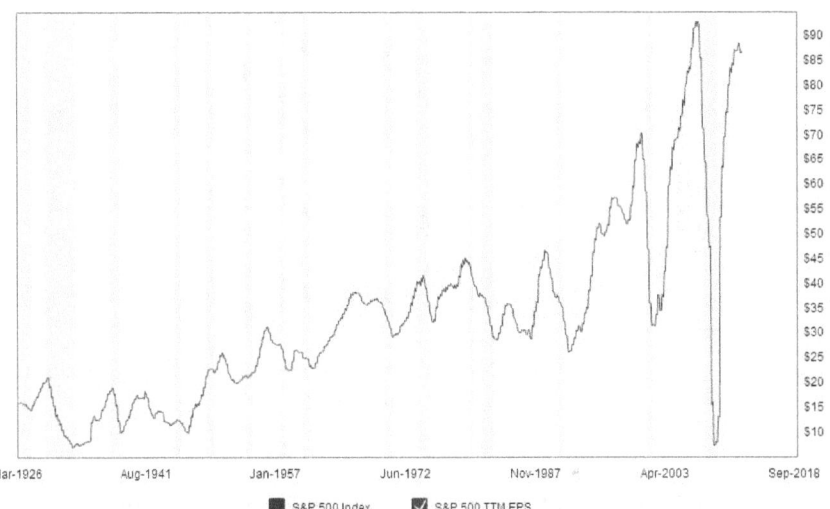

S&P 500 Earnings History - Have We Seen a Peak?

The US stock market outlook for the short term appears to be bullish, thanks to the money printing operations of the Federal Reserve (see chart below). This despite a slowing economy and many challenges to the strong growth of corporate earnings since the Financial Crisis (see chart above).

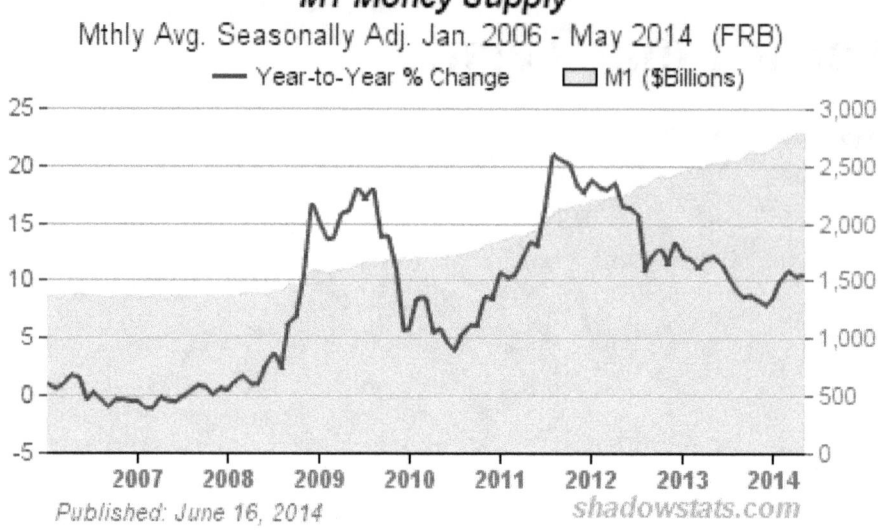

Fed Money Printing Expands the Supply of Dollars - M-1 at $2.4 Trillion (almost doubled since 2007)

While the short term outlook for stocks looks good, the longer term outlook is less clear. With the entire monetary stimulus currently being applied, the possibility of a rapid and significant rise in inflation seems more likely. Long term the dollar continues to decline in value, pushing up the value of hard assets such as gold and silver. Stocks could also benefit from inflation if companies are able to push prices faster than the increase in cost of labor and materials, which may be possible for some time after inflation becomes apparent.

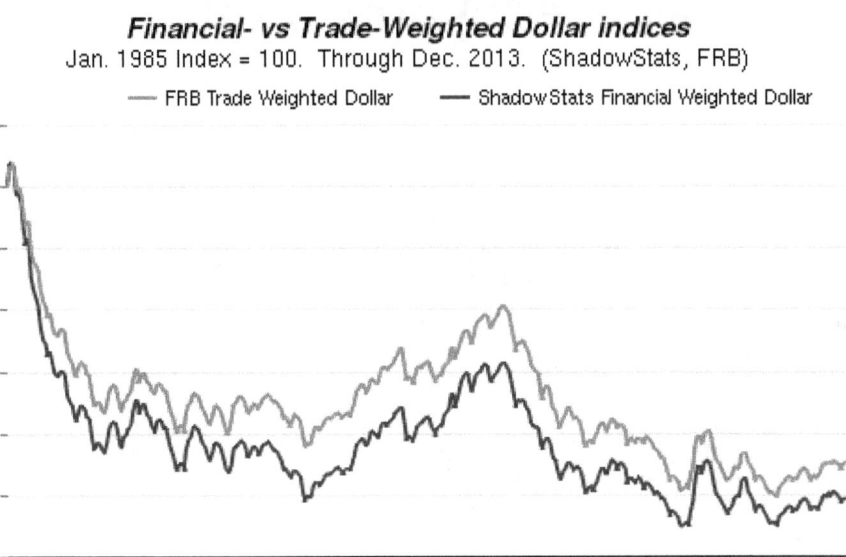

Financial- vs Trade-Weighted Dollar indices
Jan. 1985 Index = 100. Through Dec. 2013. (ShadowStats, FRB)

—— FRB Trade Weighted Dollar   —— ShadowStats Financial Weighted Dollar

Published: Dec. 31, 2013   *shadowstats.com*

Long Term Trend of the Dollar is a Significant Decline in Value

A high inflation environment will be catastrophic for bonds and will result in plummeting values as yields soar. Only those who have very short term holdings will be safe from this. Hard assets should do well in this environment, including gold and silver, real estate and oil/gas.

Time will tell, but a further decline in the value of the dollar seems unavoidable.

Land Secured Muni Bonds

2011-04-10

Municipal securities in general have suffered losses recently due to investors' fears about the finances of state and local governments. The recent bankruptcies of California cities (Stockton, Mammoth Lakes and San Bernardino) have not helped investor confidence.

One interesting type of municipal security is land-secured bonds. These are bonds issued by local agencies, such as cities or school districts for the improvement of real property (construction of infrastructure, schools, etc.). The bonds are typically secured by a property tax lien on the land benefiting from the improvements. The property tax lien is senior to any mortgage that can be placed on the property and so provides the owner of the bond with a strong probability that the principal will be repaid. Where the land is largely undeveloped, these types of bonds can be risky. However, where the land is developed or undergoing steady development and land values are stable or increasing (select sub-markets of Southern California, for example), these can be very good investments particularly as general market conditions have driven-up yields across the board. Sometimes, these types of bonds are not rated by the rating agencies (Moody's, Fitch or Standard and Poors). You need to read the "Official Statement" that accompanies each municipal bond deal to learn more about the potential risks. One key factor is the "Lien to Value Ratio" which is an indicator of how much all the tax liens on the property ("Direct and Overlapping Debt") are as a percentage of the assessed value of the property. The lower the lien to value ratio, the better.

A major advantage is that many municipal bonds are exempt from Federal taxes (including the Federal Alternative Minimum Tax) and may also be exempt from state taxes. For example, for someone who lives in California, with $150,000 of taxable income, a 7% municipal bond yield is equivalent to a 10.75% taxable yield.

If you are interested in these types of investments, Stone and Youngberg is a good source of information. They are a major trader and underwriter of municipal bond deals and they also offer trading accounts for individual investors (you may have to meet suitability qualifications first).

Shorting the Long US Treasury Bond

2011-03-27

I have been recommending a short on the long US Treasury bond for about the last six to nine months through the use of an exchange traded fund called ProShares UltraShort 20+ Year Treasury ETF (TBT), particularly when this ETF hit an all time low about 6 months ago as Treasury bond yields hit the lowest levels seen in decades. Below I have charted the spread between TBT and the Gold/Silver index. I believe the Gold/Silver index is a good indicator of future inflation expectations, which clearly have not been reflected in the long bond yield for a number of reasons. The Gold/Silver index is also an indicator of a lack of faith in paper currency, which also does not bode well for investments such as Treasury bonds. The Federal Reserve continues to intervene in the Treasury market by buying bonds, which is artificially depressing bond yields. External shocks, such as the European Sovereign Debt Crisis, the tragic disasters in Japan and war in the Middle East have caused many investors to return to the relative safety of bonds, if only temporarily, which has also helped keep bond yields down. When the Fed's intervention ends, the US Government's massive borrowing to finance persistent deficits will continue and inflation pressures also continue. These will ultimately cause the long bond yields to naturally rise from generational lows.

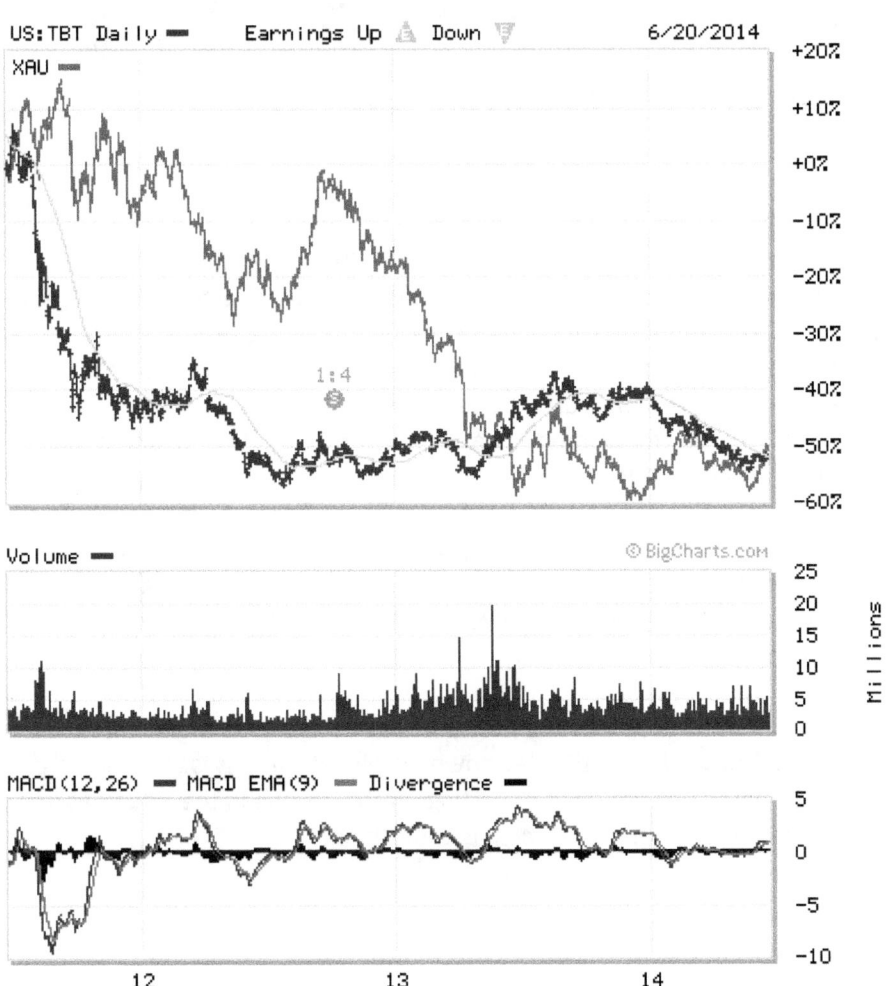

Is it Finally Time to Short Long-Term US Treasury Bonds?

2013-01-13

I have written in the past about TBT (ProShares UltraShort Lehman 20), a leveraged inverse exchange traded fund that is designed to achieve returns that are inverse to and double the increase or decrease in the 20+ year US Treasury Bond index. For example, if the index decreases 1%, this ETF should go up 2%. When the Treasury rally ends and the sell-off begins, this will be a very powerful tool to achieve outstanding returns as interest rates rise and bond prices plummet.

However as you can see in the chart below, the continuing rally in long-dated Treasury bonds since the financial crisis - Federal Reserve interest rate manipulation, "flight to safety" and investor uncertainty/fear - has resulted in a significant decline in the value of TBT.

Many investors who sensed for the past year or two that this is a "no brainer" bet have been burned by another leg down. I still believe this is the next "big short," but as with any time you are betting on the decline in the value of an asset pumped up into a bubble, timing is everything.

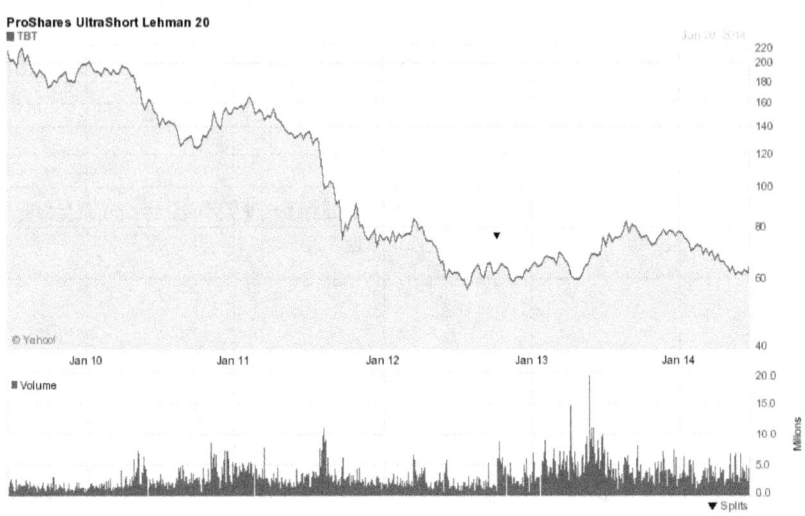

ProShares UltraShort Lehman 20
■ TBT

TBT - Time to Buy?

Why is this time any different?

Well, for one thing, more and more market observers are noticing investors putting money into stocks. For the last three weeks, equity mutual fund inflows have been almost $25 billion, far exceeding bond inflows. Many individual investors, tired of earning minimal returns in fixed income securities and seeing how well the stock market performed last year have decided to jump back into the market. Many were waiting for resolution of the "Fiscal Cliff" to do so. Also, the economic recovery, albeit weak, continues which bodes well for continued strength in the stock market.

Secondly, as I have written many times before, the easy money policies of the Federal Reserve will light the fire of inflation - it's not a question of "if" but rather "when" the inflation shows up and how much it is. While the Consumer Price Index has shown relatively benign readings lately, many believe this index is manipulated and certainly doesn't reflect reality since it excludes food and oil. The methodology of calculating the CPI has also changed over the years, resulting in lower readings that you would otherwise have if the methodology were kept constant. If you've been to the grocery store or the gas station lately, you know that these items are not getting any cheaper. As you can see in the chart below, one estimate is that we are at roughly 10% inflation now. What is more troubling is that the gap between reported and the alternate measure is widening.

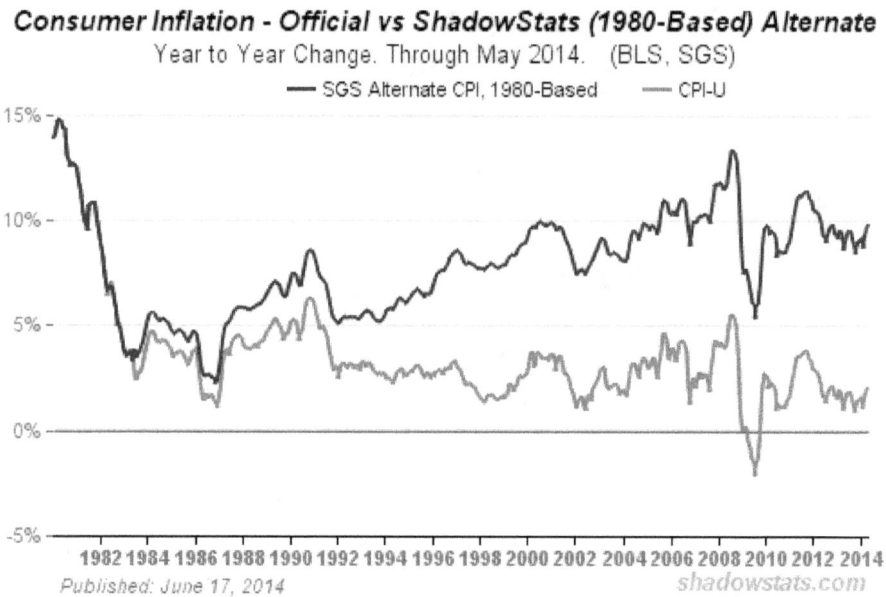

Consumer Inflation - Official vs ShadowStats (1980-Based) Alternate
Year to Year Change. Through May 2014. (BLS, SGS)
—— SGS Alternate CPI, 1980-Based   —— CPI-U

Published: June 17, 2014   shadowstats.com

The Fiscal Cliff deal hasn't addressed the annual US budget deficit or the enormous - over $16 trillion - public debt of the United States. The threat of further credit downgrades of the United States coupled with the uncertainty of any real meaningful approach to reducing the public debt will weigh on the price of Treasuries. Indeed, the easiest way to deal with the US public debt is to devalue the dollar.

Finally, the biggest concern for inflation is the huge supply of money that has been created over the past few years. There is now over $2.4 trillion in the banking system available to lend to individuals and businesses. More than $1.2 trillion has been added to the money supply since the beginning of the financial crisis (almost doubled). When this starts to go to work in the real economy, the flood of dollars will be a very powerful driver of the economy, as well as inflation.

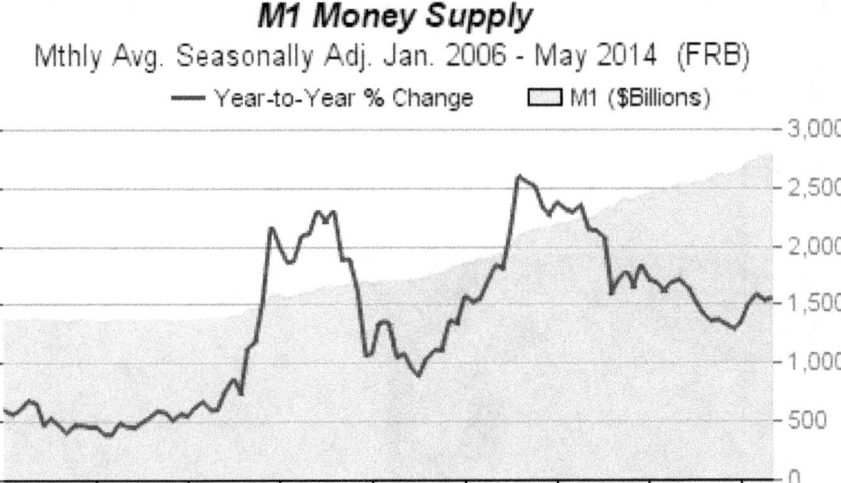

M1 Money Supply

Mthly Avg. Seasonally Adj. Jan. 2006 - May 2014 (FRB)

— Year-to-Year % Change   ☐ M1 ($Billions)

Published: June 16, 2014   shadowstats.com

I do not currently have a position in TBT.

Investing in Chinese Yuan (and Shorting the Dollar)

2012-07-14

If you believe that the dollar will lose value relative to the Chinese Yuan, as China continues to grow in economic prominence and the US economy continues to struggle, while the Fed inflates away the huge public debt burden, there are a few ETF's that offer exposure to the Chinese currency that might be worth considering.

It's no secret that China has manipulated its currency in the past, artificially lowering its value relative to the dollar to support Chinese exports. It's also no secret that China has a lot of cash now, is aggressively investing globally, is buying gold, wants to diversify away from the dollar and wants to make its currency a global reserve currency.

In fact, China has entered into agreements with its trading partners to settle directly in Chinese Yuan, including Japan, Africa and recently, Australia. This is significant because previously, all trades had to be first settled in dollars.

As you can see in the chart below, the "spread" between the rate of appreciation of the dollar and the rate of appreciation of the Yuan (I used one of the larger Yuan ETF's - CYB as a proxy for the value of the currency) has widened out significantly over the past year. It seems that in all the global turmoil and rush to US dollars and Treasury securities for "safety," the dollar has appreciated significantly over the past year and may be set for a major crash relative to the Yuan. This would especially hold true if China's economy continues to grow strongly (7.6% year over year in the quarter that just ended in June) and the US continues to grow slowly or slips back into recession.

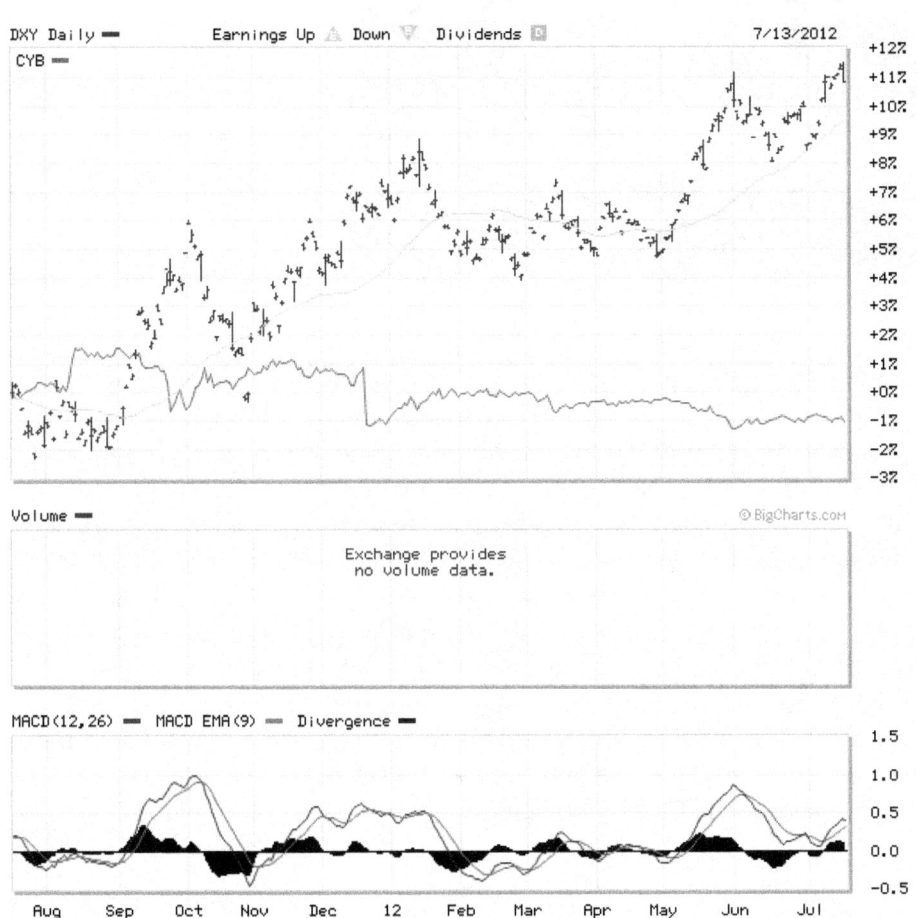

Master Limited Partnerships

2011-03-27

If you are looking for good current income and commodity upside, oil and gas limited partnerships are an excellent investment option. There is also the potential for some tax deferral of distributions. The downside is that tax reporting is more complex than other types of investments, but that's a small price to pay for the additional diversification that this investment class provides. A few of my favorite MLP's are Targa Resources Partners LP (NGLS), Vanguard Natural Resources LLC (VNR) and Linn Energy LLC (LINE). NGLS is primarily in the natural gas processing business, while VNR and LINE are in the business of acquiring and developing long-lived natural gas and oil properties. These entities hedge their exposure to commodity risk and run their businesses to maximize cash flow available to distribute to limited partners. All three of these have performed well over the past couple of years and continue to offer a dividend yields in the 6% to 7% range.

Chapter 5 - Financial Fortress - Hard Assets

2012-12-23

Building a Financial Fortress

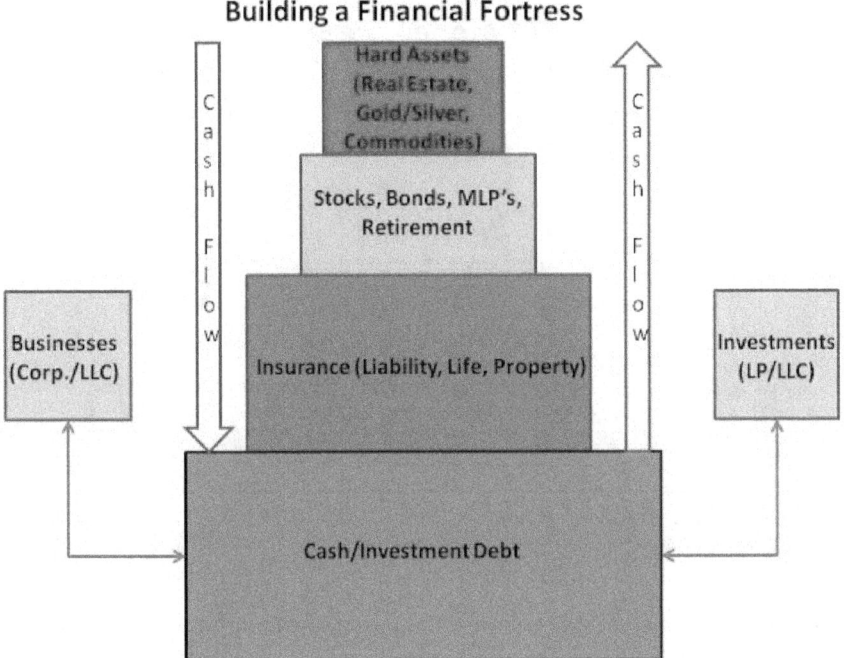

In a September 2012 post, I introduced the concept of the Financial Fortress (see graphic at right). I have published a few posts since then to explain each of the layers of the Financial Fortress, starting at the base and moving to the top.

The top of the financial fortress provides protection against inflation and consists of "hard" or "real" assets, including real estate, precious metals such as gold and silver and commodities (such as oil, natural gas, etc.). Many financial advisers are concerned about the effects of the Federal Reserve's current monetary policy, which involves the creation of a flood of new dollars to help create liquidity and stimulate the economy. The end result of this policy will be inflation - it is virtually a certainty. How much inflation and how soon it appears is really the question. The hope is that the Fed can rein the inflation in by raising interest rates and using other tools at its disposal. The chart below shows how much the money supply has grown since the beginning of the Great Recession, increasing by more than **$1 Trillion**.

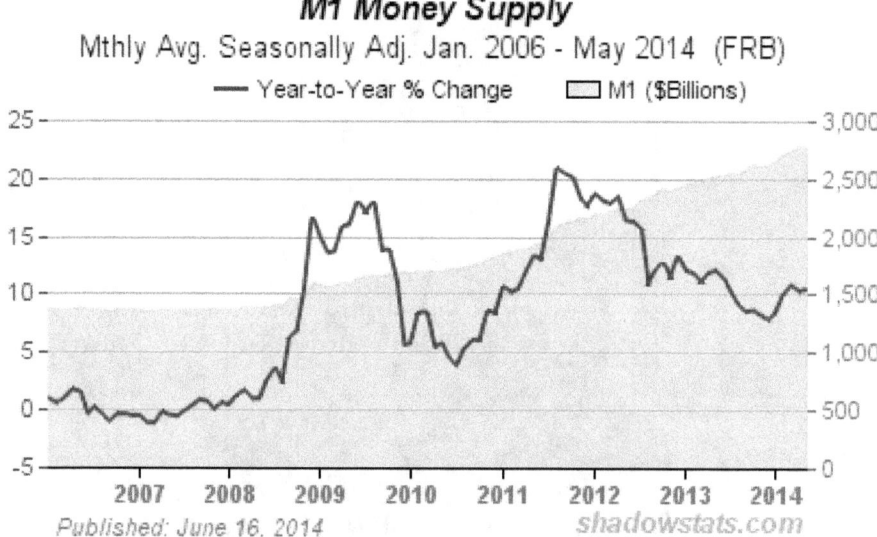

Another important chart to review is the value of the dollar. As you can see in the chart below, the value of the dollar has decreased steadily in real (inflation-adjusted terms) for many years and has lost roughly half its value since 1986:

Hard assets like gold, silver, real estate and commodities appreciate when the dollar weakens and provide a real store of value. See the 10-year charts below for gold and silver, for example:

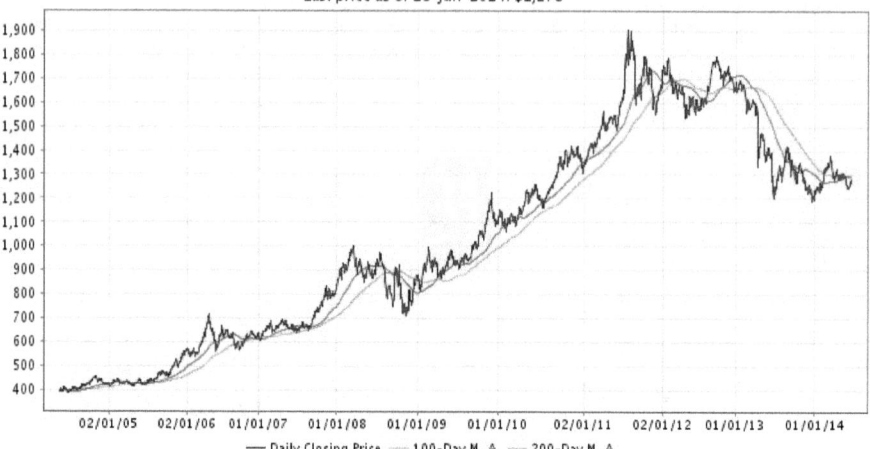

10-Year Historical Daily Closing Prices
Last price as of 18-Jun-2014: $1,278

Daily Closing Price — 100-Day M. A. — 200-Day M. A.

Gold - 10 Year Price History

10-Year Historical Daily Closing Prices
Last price as of 20-Jun-2014: $20.87

Daily Closing Price — 100-Day M. A. — 200-Day M. A.

Silver - 10 Year Price History

Since the value of silver and gold is expressed in dollars, devaluation of the dollar tends to drive up the value of these and other precious metals.

I recommend buying gold and silver in physical form, bars or coins, and storing them in a bank safe deposit box or vault. You can also buy shares in gold or silver exchange traded funds and also buy stocks of mining companies, but I prefer to hold the physical asset for greater control and certainty.

The best way to invest in oil and gas, I have found, is through publicly traded master limited partnerships (see related blog post on this topic). These provide high current yield and have tax advantages (tax free distributions until your initial investment is recovered).

Real estate requires a bit more work, particularly when identifying suitable investment property (a topic which I have posted on regularly). If you run it like a business and ensure you purchase a property that can provide positive cash flow, there are few better investments than real estate particularly with the leverage you are able to enjoy with a mortgage.

Hopefully, you will be able to build your own financial fortress, if you haven't already started, before the next financial crisis is upon us.

The Real Value of Hard Assets

2011-04-02

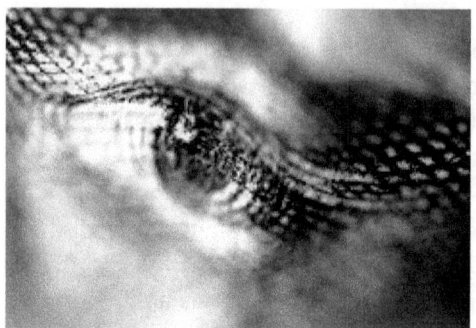

I advocate <u>investing</u> in hard <u>assets</u> (gold, silver, <u>real estate</u>, oil/gas, etc.). You only have to look at the <u>grocery store</u> or the gas station to see why. Inflation is clearly happening all around us, yet the official government statistics don't show it. Did you ever wonder why the <u>Consumer Price Index</u> or CPI doesn't track with your experience? For one thing, CPI excludes food and energy costs - officially because these items are volatile and can skew the index, but these are the very things that people buy every day. Beyond that does the official measure of unemployment track with what you know is happening in your community to people you know, friends and family? The real <u>rate of unemployment</u> in this country is most likely north of 20% versus the official measure of just under 10%. The charts below depict intriguing alternative measures of annual consumer <u>inflation</u> and unemployment for your consideration. It's interesting to note the divergence in the alternative measure versus the official measure over time.

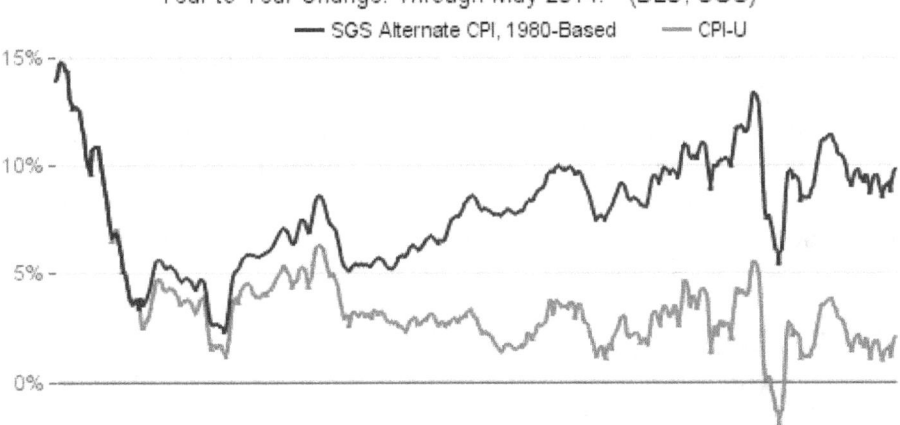

Consumer Inflation - Official vs ShadowStats (1980-Based) Alternate
Year to Year Change. Through May 2014. (BLS, SGS)
— SGS Alternate CPI, 1980-Based   — CPI-U

Published: June 17, 2014   shadowstats.com

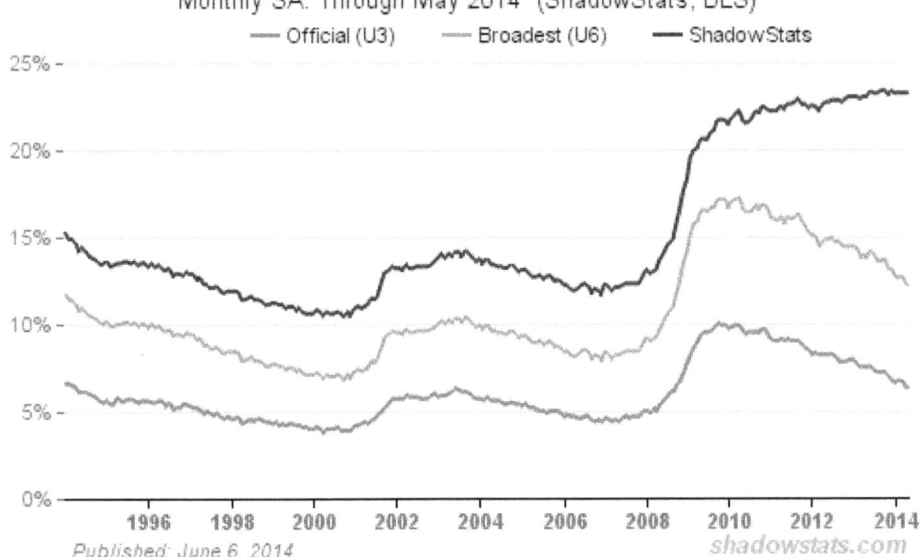

Unemployment Rate - Official (U-3 & U-6) vs ShadowStats Alternate
Monthly SA. Through May 2014 (ShadowStats, BLS)
— Official (U3)   — Broadest (U6)   — ShadowStats

Published: June 6, 2014   shadowstats.com

Another investment theme, which is linked to inflation concerns, is the continued deterioration in the value of the dollar. With the government printing more dollars every day (so-called quantitative easing), the decline in the value of the dollar has accelerated - this worsens inflation and diminishes the purchasing power of dollar denominated assets (like your savings account). The chart below shows the long-term decline in the value of the dollar and suggests that official reports understate the true decline in the dollar index. Indeed, some are concerned that we may experience hyperinflation in the United States before too long. If you are interested in this subject, I highly recommend two books I have read recently that help explain what is happening and how to protect yourself as an investor:

Financial- vs Trade-Weighted Dollar indices
Jan. 1985 Index = 100. Through Dec. 2013. (ShadowStats, FRB)

Published: Dec. 31, 2013   shadowstats.com

Ironically, in an inflationary environment with a <u>declining dollar</u>, the best position is to be a long-term borrower and investor in hard assets. Real estate works best, since you can still get a 30-year fixed loan for 4% to 5% (on investment property) today, which will be repaid in devalued dollars, while the value of the property appreciates due to inflation. Most people claim they do not want to be in debt at all, but that misses the point that there is both "<u>good debt</u>" and "bad debt." I define "bad debt" as loans to buy things you consume - even your primary residence, because these things do not earn a return on your investment. "Good debt" would include a mortgage on an investment property, assuming the property provides you with positive cash flow each month.

Quote of the Day - Penny for your thoughts

2012-09-12

Ever notice how it's a penny for your thoughts, yet you put in your two cents? Someone is making a penny on the deal! — Stephen Wright

Hard Assets for Hard Times

2011-04-22

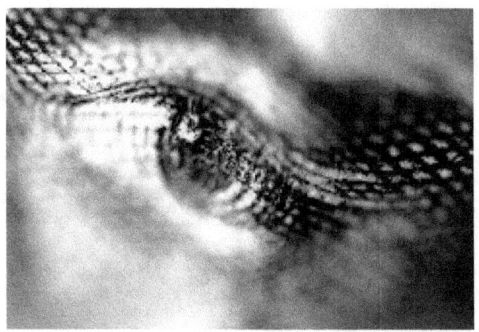

If you want to protect your family and your wealth, it seems like the best place to invest now and in the foreseeable future is in hard assets: i.e., gold, silver, oil, commodities and real estate.

Although the stock market has been doing well recently, we all know that it is a rigged game run for the benefit of institutions. Many people lost most of their savings when the stock market crashed in 2008/2009. I wouldn't want to have a significant portion of my wealth in the stock market now or anytime in the future.

The bond market isn't much better. Having enjoyed a long bull market, the weight of the US government's borrowing coupled with inflationary fears are driving investors away. The smart money (Warren Buffett, Bill Gross) are selling U.S. Treasuries and I have been recommending a long US Treasury shorting strategy using a leveraged Exchange Traded Fund - Proshares UltraShort 20+ Year Treasury ETF (TBT) that has done pretty well over the past six months.

Real estate has been out of favor for the past few years, but provides an excellent hedge against inflation and the advantage of leveraging long-term borrowed funds at a fixed interest rate.

Hard assets have real tangible value and have benefited tremendously from the destruction of the dollar's value - a direct result of the <u>Federal Reserve</u> keeping <u>interest rates</u> at almost zero and <u>printing money</u> in order to shore-up the economy (see the chart below showing the <u>US Dollar index</u> for the past 10 years).

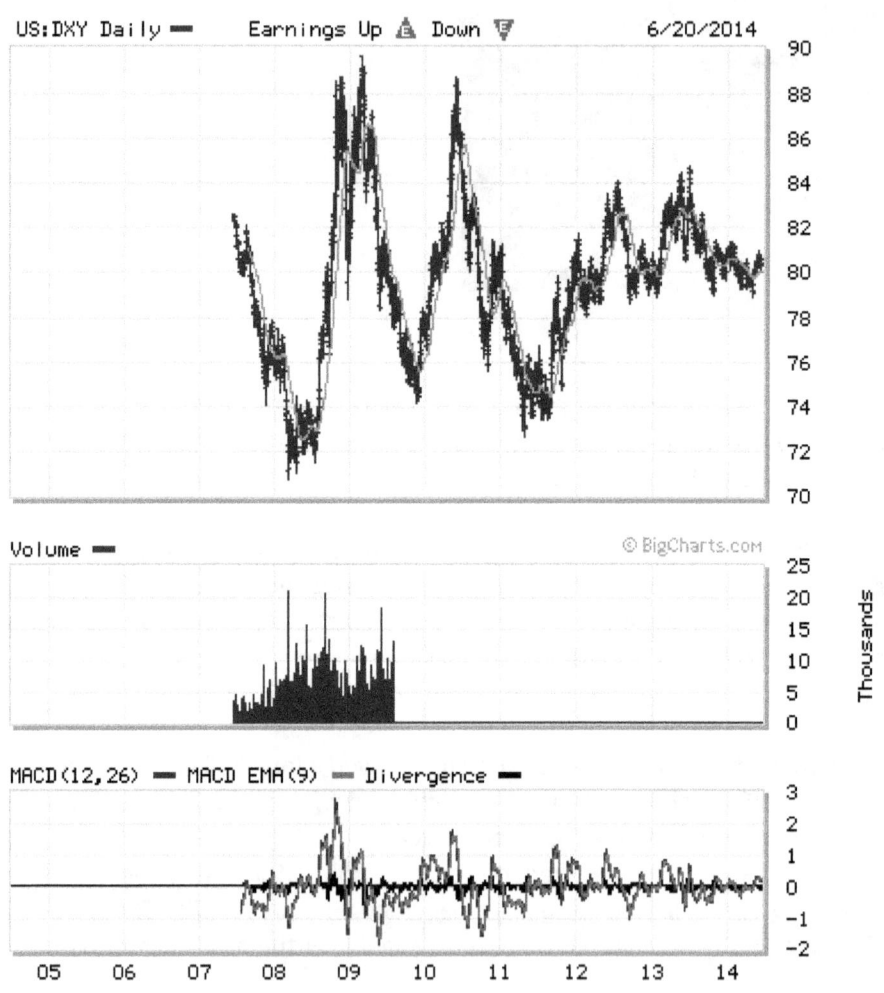

The government's ability to continue to borrow to finance <u>massive deficits</u> is nearing an end. As was widely reported this week, rating agencies have placed a negative outlook on US sovereign debt. If the government is serious about reducing the public debt, a major correction has yet to occur - higher taxes and lower government spending could slow economic growth enough to put the United States back into recession. The alternative is a US sovereign default, a far more serious outcome which would result in financial market chaos accompanied by a collapse of the dollar and social unrest.

An interesting side note - this is all coming to pass almost exactly how Rich Dad (Robert Kiyosaki) called it in Conspiracy of the Rich.

Gold vs Silver

2011-03-27

I like to study the relationship between the price of gold and silver. I review the charts for two popular exchange traded funds to do this - IShares Silver Trust ETF (SLV) and SPDR Gold ETF (GLD). In the past, I recommended the purchase of silver, especially when silver's rate of appreciation was trailing gold by a significant margin - approximately six months ago. As you can see in the chart, not only has silver closed the gap, its level of appreciation has greatly exceeded gold. That would indicate that either silver is now overpriced or gold is underpriced and needs to catch up. I wouldn't recommend adding to silver investments at this time.

Is Silver Really Ready for a Crash?

2011-04-30

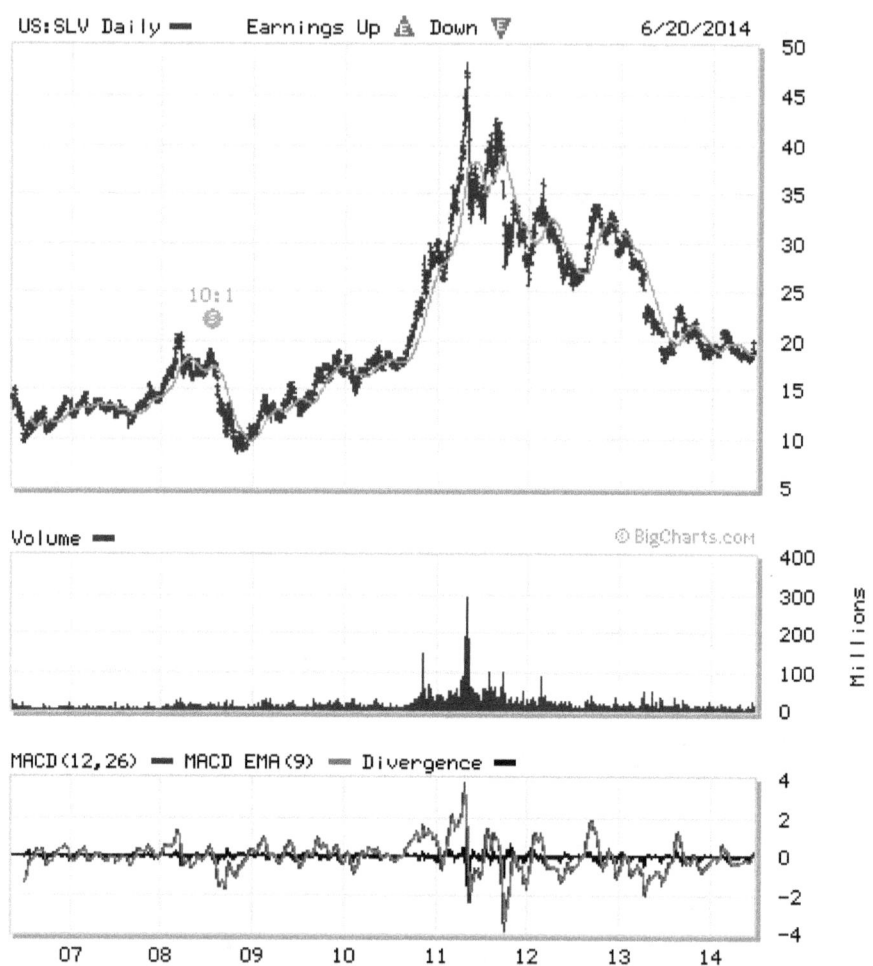

As shown in the chart above for the iShares Silver Trust ETF (SLV), silver has enjoyed a parabolic rise in value over the past few months, recently closing at close to $50/share (one share is roughly equivalent to an ounce of silver). The previous nominal high reached in the 1980's was about $50/ounce. Many people are beginning to say that silver is ready to crash and a few bloggers have even suggested that now might be good time to short silver. I would much rather short the long US Treasury Bond using ProShares UltraShort 20+ Year Treasury ETF (TBT) than to try to short silver right now.

Here are the long term fundamentals for silver:

- Federal Reserve continues to print money, keep interest rates artificially low and thereby debase the currency, increasing the value of hard assets such as gold and silver
- The creditworthiness of the United States and the reserve currency status of the US dollar are no longer unquestionable - as shown in the chart below, the long-term trend for the dollar is a decline in value
- Prior peak inflation-adjusted value of silver is conservatively $150/ounce, which would indicate that silver has a little more room to run
- Silver is consumed in industrial applications, unlike gold which never "goes away"
- Silver is much more affordable than gold, making it accessible to more individual investors

Building A Financial Fortress

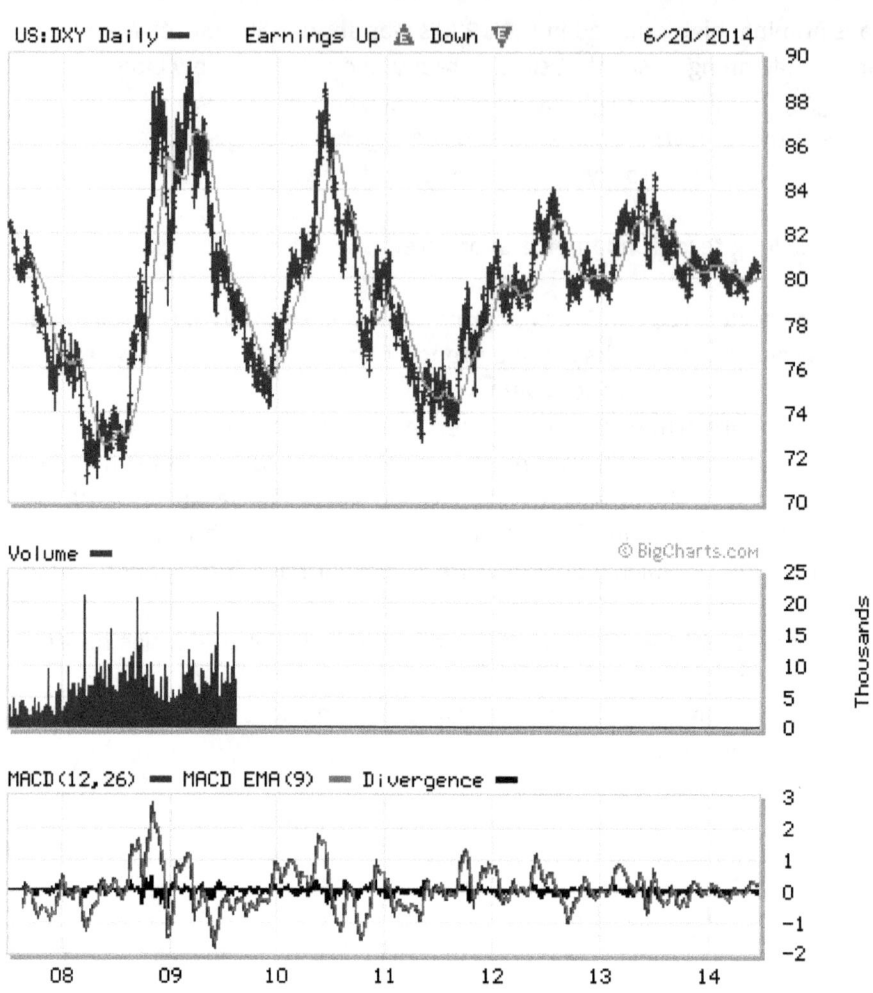

Why I Still Like Gold and Silver

2012-07-04

5-Year Historical Daily Closing Prices
Last price as of 20-Jun-2014: $1,315

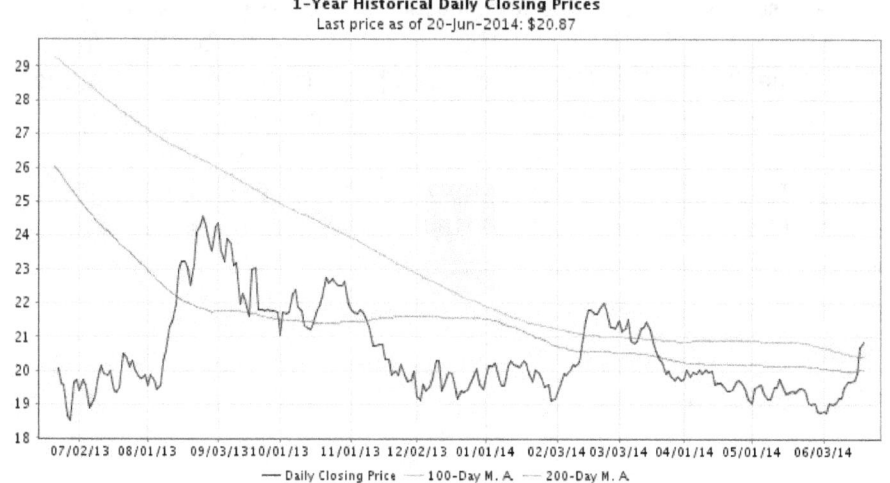

1-Year Historical Daily Closing Prices
Last price as of 20-Jun-2014: $20.87

Building A Financial Fortress

Recently, I have read many articles that are calling a "top" in gold and silver. The charts at right might lead one to believe that the speculation has run its course and that these metals are headed lower. Indeed, one particularly bearish article suggested that gold will drop to $500 - $700 an ounce within a year. Certainly, the investment performance of gold and silver so far this year has been uninspiring. I can also understand how gold and silver can experience near term weakness in the face of panic selling (similar to what we saw in 2007/2008 at the peak of the financial crisis), when all investors were seeking liquidity at any cost and were buying short term US treasuries and selling everything else. We could certainly see more of that type of selling as Europe's issues continue to unfold.

As it relates to Europe's troubles, there is really only one politically expedient way for Europe to bail out their banks (make no mistake, Greece and Spain are only the beginning - see the table below that shows bank leverage) and to try to pull the Euro zone out of recession - massive liquidity injections by Central Banks including interest rate cuts and bond buying.

Indeed, the Federal Reserve will undoubtedly need to stay the same course in the coming months as inflation appears to be tame and the US economy continues to teeter on the brink of recession. The US will have its own sovereign debt crisis to deal with in the not too distant future, as the public debt already surpasses $15 trillion and unfunded liabilities (social security, Medicare, etc.) exceed $119 trillion! There is no other option but to inflate away the value of these liabilities by devaluing paper currencies! As such, the medium and long term prospects for real money such as gold and silver have never looked better. Also, investors who use leverage at low fixed rates to acquire assets that generate dependable cash flow streams (i.e., real estate) will also benefit greatly from the coming inflation.

The Case for Gold and Silver

2012-09-07

Yesterday, the European Central Bank announced that it would not limit the amount of bonds it would purchase from Spain and Italy, which immediately caused the interest rates on Spanish and Italian bonds to drop and markets everywhere rallied. This was a bold step, but one that continues to reinforce what all countries are seeking to do to avert crisis and ensure stability: print money and keep borrowing rates artificially low. Gold is now trading close to $1,700/ounce and silver is trading close to $33/ounce as the precious metals continue to be favored by investors who are uncertain about the future and are worried about inflation from the monetary operations of the European Central Bank and our own Federal Reserve. Bernanke has clearly signaled the Fed's concern about unemployment and their willingness to continue to keep interest rates low, even if it means using "unconventional" policy tools:

As we assess the benefits and costs of alternative policy approaches, though, we must not lose sight of the daunting economic challenges that confront our nation. The stagnation of the labor market in particular is a grave concern not only because of the enormous suffering and waste of human talent it entails, but also because persistently high levels of unemployment will wreak structural damage on our economy that could last for many years.

Over the past five years, the Federal Reserve has acted to support economic growth and foster job creation, and it is important to achieve further progress, particularly in the labor market. Taking due account of the uncertainties and limits of its policy tools, the Federal Reserve will provide additional policy accommodation as needed to promote a stronger economic recovery and sustained improvement in labor market conditions in a context of price stability.

Gold Chart:

Silver Chart:

10-Year Historical Daily Closing Prices
Last price as of 20-Jun-2014: $20.87

Daily Closing Price — 100-Day M. A. — 200-Day M. A.

Some believe that gold and silver cannot continue to rise in value, and yet they have consistently over a long period of time (silver, of course, is much more volatile). Many investors believe that with the entire world printing money, the value of gold and silver could double or triple in the next year. I could be wrong, but I think the truth is probably somewhere in the middle and gold and silver will continue to steadily increase in value over time. Investors should have a portion of their portfolio in precious metals, preferably physical gold and silver (Silver Eagle and Gold American Buffalo bullion coins produced by the US Mint are excellent ways to invest).

Since 1985, the value of the dollar has declined by half. This will continue to provide fuel to the value of gold and silver:

Financial- vs Trade-Weighted Dollar indices
Jan. 1985 Index = 100. Through Dec. 2013. (ShadowStats, FRB)

—— FRB Trade Weighted Dollar   —— ShadowStats Financial Weighted Dollar

Published: Dec. 31, 2013

shadowstats.com

Four Reasons to Continue to Invest in Gold and Silver

2012-10-06

Although there has been some recent price weakness, gold and silver continue to shine for investors, as shown in the charts below:

5-Year Historical Daily Closing Prices
Last price as of 20-Jun-2014: $1,315

5-Year Historical Daily Closing Prices
Last price as of 20-Jun-2014: $20.87

— Daily Closing Price   — 100-Day M. A   — 200-Day M. A

Here are four reasons why it's still smart to have at least some of your assets invested in gold and silver:

1) <u>The Dollar</u> - Dollar continues to decline in value as a result of continued easy money policy/money printing by the <u>Federal Reserve</u>. This trend seems unlikely to reverse any time soon based on recent Fed policy statements. Noteworthy: the dollar has lost about half of its <u>purchasing power</u> since 1986.

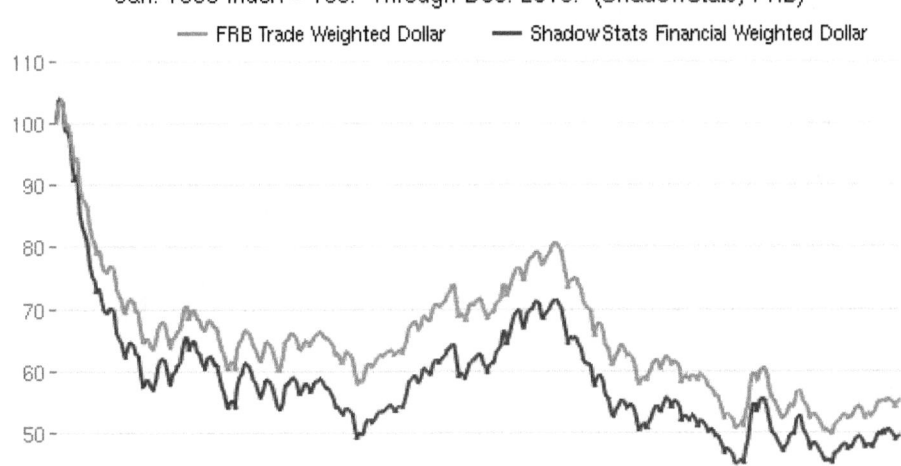

Financial- vs Trade-Weighted Dollar indices
Jan. 1985 Index = 100. Through Dec. 2013. (ShadowStats, FRB)

— FRB Trade Weighted Dollar   — ShadowStats Financial Weighted Dollar

Published: Dec. 31, 2013   shadowstats.com

2) <u>Inflation</u> - Actual rate of inflation is likely higher than reported rate and official statistics show continued weakness in <u>employment</u> growth, as noted below from the <u>September unemployment report</u>:

Total nonfarm payroll employment increased by 114,000 in September. In2012, employment growth has averaged 146,000 per month, compared with an average monthly gain of 153,000 in 2011.

Critical items such as food and fuel are excluded from the official measure due to volatility but these continue to increase, having a greater impact on the middle class and poor.

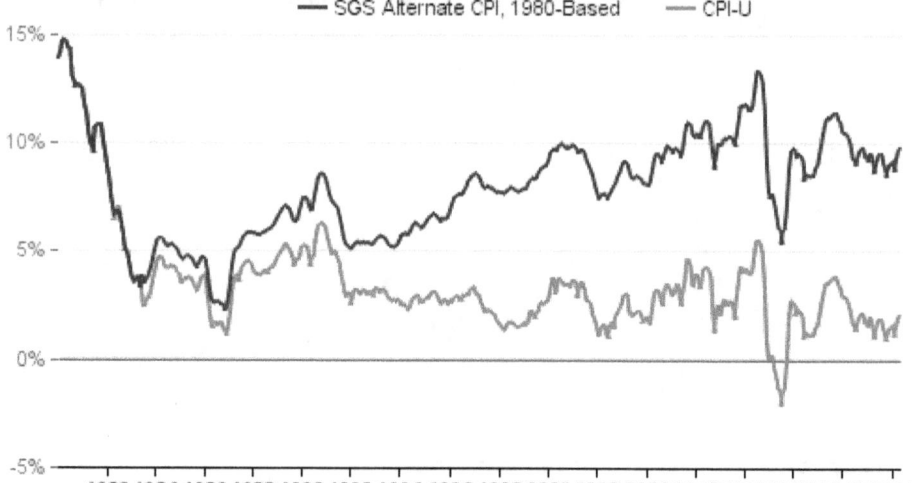

Consumer Inflation - Official vs ShadowStats (1980-Based) Alternate
Year to Year Change. Through May 2014.   (BLS, SGS)

—— SGS Alternate CPI, 1980-Based   —— CPI-U

Published: June 17, 2014   shadowstats.com

3) <u>Unemployment</u> - A hotly debated topic lately, the official rate <u>recently reported</u> is 7.8% but alternate data which includes those "discouraged" individuals who are no longer seeking work has continued to rise and is approaching 25%. **Noteworthy:** The U.S. has only recovered 4.2 million of the 8.8 million jobs lost during the <u>Great Recession</u>!

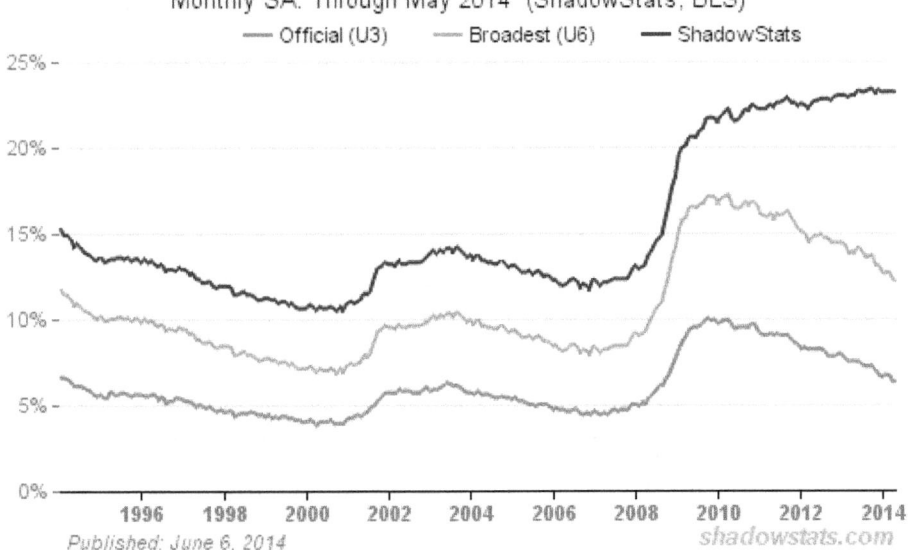

Unemployment Rate - Official (U-3 & U-6) vs ShadowStats Alternate
Monthly SA. Through May 2014 (ShadowStats, BLS)
—— Official (U3)   —— Broadest (U6)   —— ShadowStats

Published: June 6, 2014

shadowstats.com

4) **Money Supply** - If you look at M-1 (includes cash/coins in circulation and checking accounts), although the rate of growth has slowed, the total amount of money in circulation has grown almost $1 trillion since 2008, almost double! This is significant and does not bode well for inflation or value of the dollar.

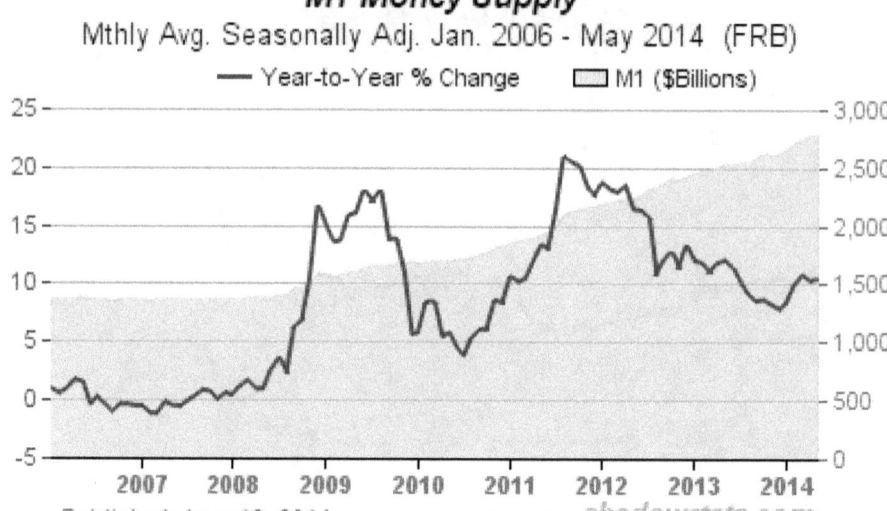

M1 Money Supply
Mthly Avg. Seasonally Adj. Jan. 2006 - May 2014 (FRB)
— Year-to-Year % Change   □ M1 ($Billions)

Published: June 16, 2014   shadowstats.com

Recession is when a neighbor loses his job. Depression is when you lose yours.
Ronald Reagan

Asset Class Review: Precious Metals Are Looking Attractive Again

2014-06-01

Looking at the different types of investments available, stocks seem overvalued at the current market levels, so it's difficult to put new money there unless you have identified a particular company that looks poised for growth. Even then, it probably makes sense to trim your stock market exposure and remain broadly diversified. Bonds are worrisome with the threat of higher interest rates; however it looks like until the economy gets going and unemployment becomes less of an issue, the Fed will continue to keep rates low, which bodes well for borrowers; okay for bond investors who can at least earn a modest yield. Real estate seems to be enjoying a nice run-up in most markets, but is getting pricey. Precious metals had a tough year last year, but they are beginning to look like a buy.

Silver is looking very attractive at current prices of $18.80 per ounce and recently touching a low not seen in a year (see chart below). The investment thesis is still sound: the metal is consumed in industrial applications so as the economy improves so does demand. Also, silver has safe haven appeal and protection against declining value of the dollar, which even at low rates of inflation steadily erodes over time. A dollar now only buys about half of what it did in 1985, for example (see chart below).

5-Year Historical Daily Closing Prices
Last price as of 20-Jun-2014: $20.87

— Daily Closing Price — 100-Day M. A. — 200-Day M. A.

Financial- vs Trade-Weighted Dollar indices
Jan. 1985 Index = 100. Through Dec. 2013. (ShadowStats, FRB)

— FRB Trade Weighted Dollar   — ShadowStats Financial Weighted Dollar

Published: Dec. 31, 2013   shadowstats.com

Gold is looking good as well (see chart below) and so is investment thesis as timeless store of value, safe haven and inflation hedge.

5-Year Historical Daily Closing Prices
Last price as of 20-Jun-2014: $1,315

Although government statistics seem to say inflation is low and even "below target" from the Fed's point of view, the real story on inflation unfolds when you go to the gas station or grocery store, buy a car or pay rent.

Consumer Inflation - Official vs ShadowStats (1980-Based) Alternate
Year to Year Change. Through May 2014. (BLS, SGS)
— SGS Alternate CPI, 1980-Based   — CPI-U

Published: June 17, 2014   shadowstats.com

Other investment alternatives worth considering include early stage investing through a crowd funding site. These do require you to be an accredited investor (i.e., net worth not including home over $1 million or earning more than $200K/year) and initial investment can be substantial and risk of loss is very high. If you have available funds, investing in one or two well-researched crowd funding deals could add a nice lift to your portfolio down the road if the company is successful. There are several crowd funding sites but only a few that allow you to invest for a return (vs. make a donation to a cause). One of the premier sites is Crowdfunder.

Disclosure: I own physical gold and silver as part of a broadly diversified investment portfolio.

Before You Sell Commodities, Take a Deep Breath

2011-05-08

I have been reading a lot lately about all the "dumb money" that bought silver, gold and oil in the weeks preceding last week's cratering of the commodities markets. Apparently, the "smart money" was selling when everyone else (i.e., retail investors) were buying. I find the whole "smart money/dumb money" thing offensive. Either you are an educated investor or not. The only difference in my mind is whether you can gamble with other people's money (or in the case of large institutions, using money borrowed from the Fed for virtually zero interest).

After last week, you may be thinking about selling gold, silver, oil and other commodity holdings and getting back into the stock market or bond market (or even holding cash). Take a deep breath. The strategy of investing in commodities for the long term is fundamentally sound. The chart below shows the consumer price index and annual rate of inflation since 1985. **The dollar has lost approximately half of its purchasing power in that time frame as a result of inflation**:

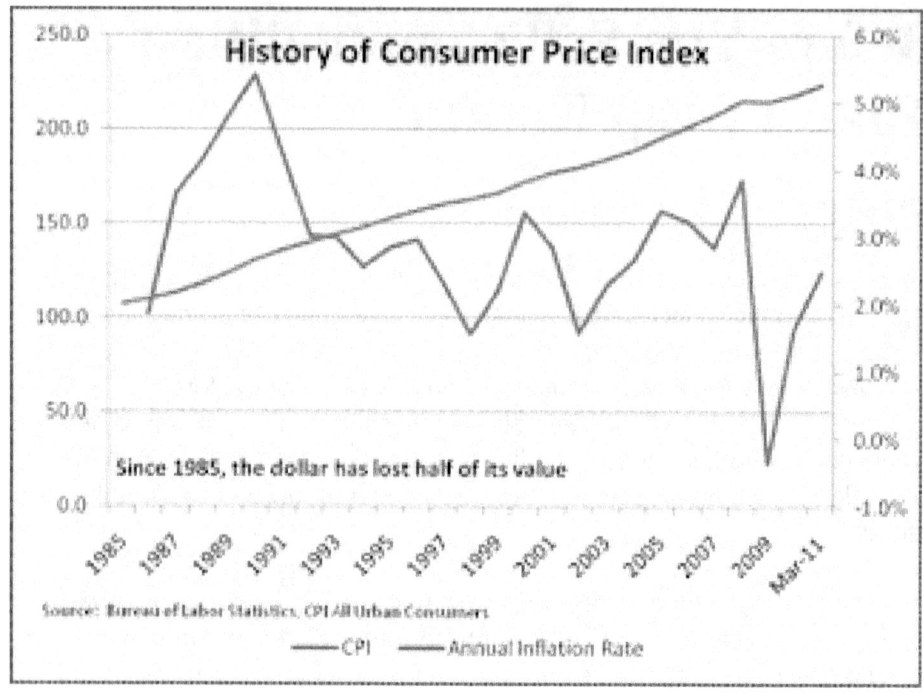

Gold, on the other hand, has increased in value 400% in that period (from $300/oz to $1,500/oz).

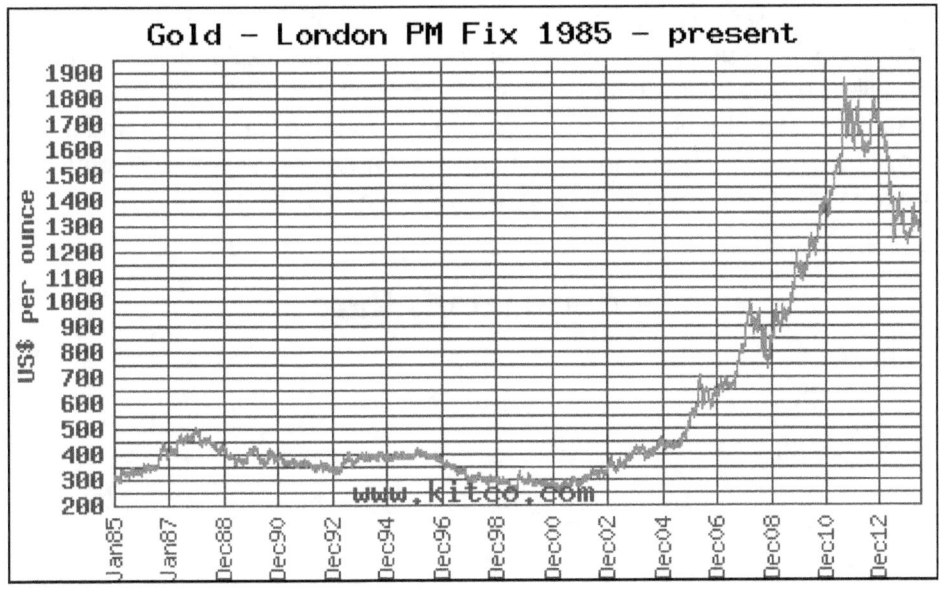

Silver increased approximately 300% from $9/oz to $36/oz (400% when silver was at $45/oz).

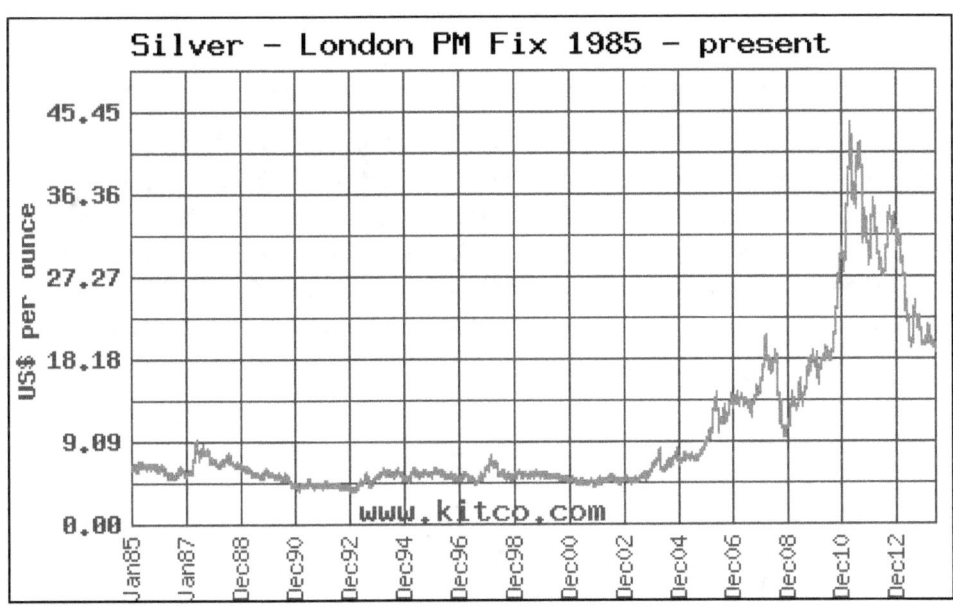

Building A Financial Fortress

The Federal Reserve is on a mission to devalue the dollar, which means more inflation and less purchasing power for your dollars. By keeping interest rates virtually zero and buying bonds on the open market, the Fed is accomplishing its goal. The Fed is also helping their pals in the investment/banking community by providing plenty of cheap money to borrow (in fact, the money has become progressively cheaper since 1985, as shown in the chart below):

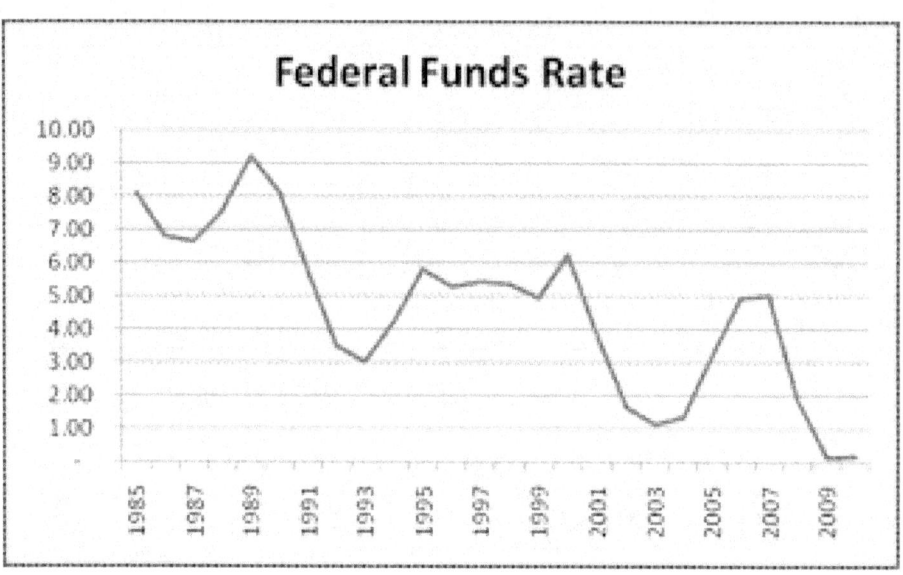

As for investing in stocks, be careful. The Dow Jones Industrial Average is up over 30% in the past year and has almost doubled since hitting an all time low during the financial crisis in 2009. The same is true of the NASDAQ and the S&P 500. Many people believe the stock market could experience another "flash crash" again, or worse. Let's also not forget the "lost decade" for the S&P 500, where there has been virtually no return to investors who are broadly invested in stocks:

Building A Financial Fortress

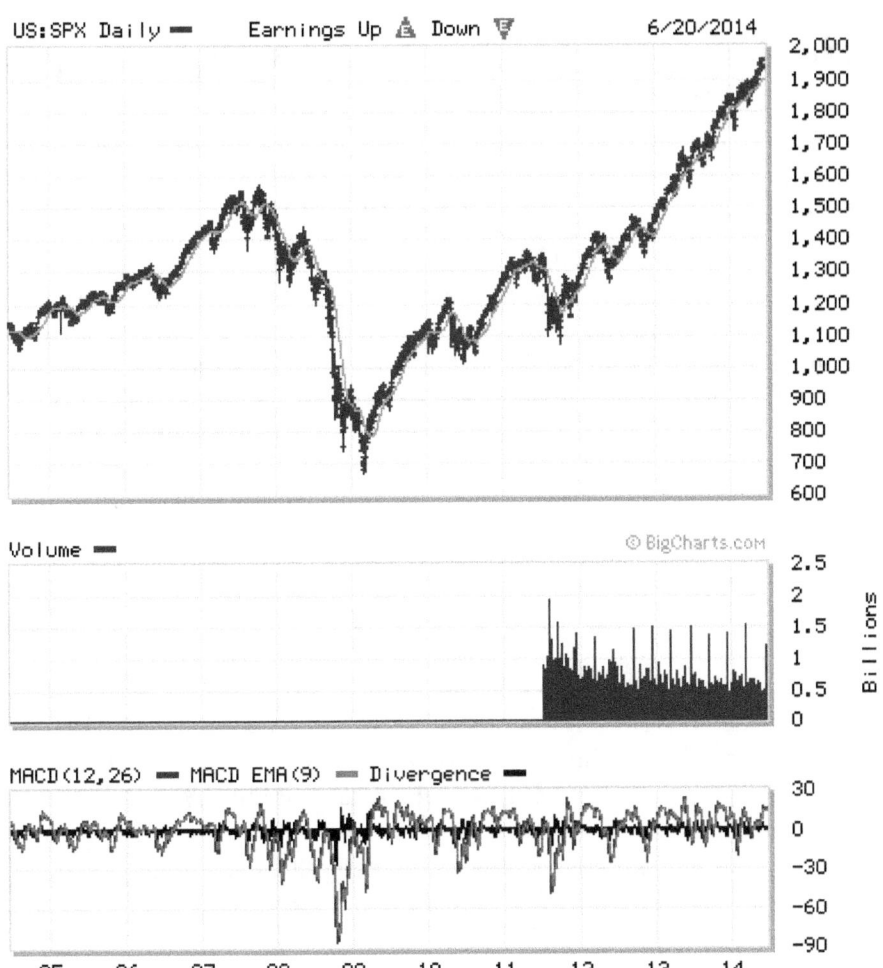

Stay the course. A well diversified portfolio includes commodities, as well as real estate and other assets.

Your House is Not An Asset - Part II

2011-05-29

As Robert Kiyosaki (Rich Dad, Poor Dad author) says, "Your House is Not An Asset." This is because your house takes money out of your pocket each and every month for the mortgage, property taxes, HOA dues, repairs, etc. Investment property, if it is cash flow positive, is an asset because it puts cash into your pocket every month. A bigger house is not better - only more expensive.

Now here is some news that you may find chilling, especially if you are a homeowner in the most expensive markets of the United States, such as the East or West coast.

The White House has recently announced plans to restructure Fannie Mae and Freddie Mac (which currently buy almost all of the mortgages originated in the United States). This would restrict and potentially eliminate the government's role in the housing finance system. This could mean that the days of the 30-year fixed rate mortgage are numbered, or at least that the days of low rates for these types of loans are numbered. The fact is, without a government guarantee, very few private investors would want to own a 30-year mortgage.

As if that weren't bad enough, Congress is struggling with the massive federal debt and is looking for ways to raise taxes. One of the ways Congress is looking at raising taxes is to modify the deductibility of mortgage interest (which is one of the highest tax expenditure items at $88.7 billion annually). What's more, the Tax Foundation's take on the mortgage interest deduction is that it really only benefits the real estate industry and doesn't increase home ownership:

Economists find that the MID gets capitalized into the price of homes and may amplify price volatility,[3]which offsets whatever effect it has on promoting home ownership. The actual economic benefits of those capitalized costs tend to flow to the home builders and realtors, who have naturally been the most vocal opponents of eliminating the MID. One study determined that the MID is "an ineffective policy to promote homeownership and improve social welfare."[4]

While the lion's share of the blame for the current housing crisis properly rests with government-sponsored enterprises Fannie Mae and Freddie Mac, the MID certainly played a role in encouraging some families to purchase homes that they really could not have afforded otherwise. Canada does not have a mortgage interest deduction, yet its rate of homeownership is equal to that in the U.S. Even the *Washington Post* has editorialized that it is time to "[t]rim the excessive tax subsidy for real estate."[5]

There are several proposals being considered, including eliminating the deduction altogether, "capping" the maximum mortgage amount at $500,000 (currently $1,000,000), eliminating the deductibility of Home Equity Lines of Credit (currently up to $100,000 if used to acquire or improve your primary residence) and/or potentially providing a tax credit of 12% instead of a tax deduction for mortgage interest. For anyone with a mortgage over $500,000 who is underwater, this could mean the difference between staying in the home or finally handing the keys over to the lender. As you can see in the table below, in the "Cap with Credit" scenario, it would cost a homeowner with a $765,000 mortgage with a 35% marginal tax rate over $1,000 more per month to continue to own their home because of the lost tax benefit. Those with higher mortgage balances (and higher marginal tax rates) will be even worse off. This would potentially be a boon to the entry level buyer, especially under the "Cap with Credit" scenario if they don't itemize their deductions (they now get the tax credit, which is a dollar for dollar reduction in their tax liability).
Everyone should pay close attention to this debate as it unfolds in the coming months.

Building A Financial Fortress

	Current Law	$500K "Cap"	$500K "Cap" w/Credit
Mortgage	$765,000	$500,000	$500,000
Interest	6%	6%	6%
Annual Interest Deduction	$45,900	$30,000	$30,000
Tax/Credit Rate	35%	35%	12%
Tax Benefit	$16,065	$10,500	$3,600
Additional Annual Cost		*$5,565*	*$12,465*

Timeshare (Vacation Ownership) - A Prepaid Vacation, Not An Investment!

2012-08-29

I'm just back from a trip to Hawaii and we had a great time there visiting family and relaxing. While staying at our resort, I was reminded that the timeshare industry is alive and well there. You will often hear people say how great it is to own a timeshare in Hawaii since it is in such high demand and you can exchange your week(s) for just about any place in the world easily. That's really cool if 1) you can actually get regular vacation time each year for one or two weeks, 2) you can find a suitable place to "exchange" into each year, or if not 3) you are happy returning to the exact same place year after year. The thing you have to remember is that timeshare (also called vacation ownership) is really pretty simple: it's a prepaid vacation. If you return to the same place year after year it might make sense, but why own when you can rent? We just stayed in a different place than we have for the past few years and it was terrific - great amenities for the whole family (sandy beach, pool with a waterfall/water slide and a poolside bar serving Kona Brewing Company beer on tap - check!). I have really enjoyed our vacations at timeshare resorts - you book your trip online, find a good deal and away you go. If you can manage to avoid the "free" breakfast, you don't have to sit through the presentation and high-pressure sales pitch.

Don't believe the timeshare sales agent when they say this is investing in real estate - it's not. You own a fractional interest in a unit, it's true, and you may even be able to deduct the interest on the loan (assuming you don't pay cash), but you are on the hook for your proportionate share of all costs of ownership (including insurance, property taxes, homeowner association, etc.). In addition, you are also responsible for your proportionate interest in a vacation ownership association, which runs the front desk, housekeeping, maintenance of the units, etc. This can be quite costly and as an individual owner you have very little control over these costs. Reselling your timeshare can also be a nightmare - the resale market is generally loaded with units that are often priced below the developer's pricing (all the more reason not to buy from the developer).

You might think owning a "condo tel" is better since you actually own an entire unit and when you aren't using it, the hotel rents it out to individual travelers and you get a share of the revenue (after covering all costs, of course). Unfortunately, these are much better for the developer (who gets to cash out by selling the units to individuals) and the operator who gets to run a hotel without having to own the hotel. As a unit owner, you are exposed to all ownership/proportionate hotel operating costs of the unit and if there are no visitors, you are likely to incur a sizable loss each month. Not only that, but resale of these units will be a challenge since the buyer pool is limited (some units have very small or no kitchen - just like a hotel room).

If you really like taking vacations, stay in a condo or hotel - even if it's a timeshare operation, just avoid the free breakfast and/or the discounted tour/luau tickets.

If you really want to invest in real estate, then buy an investment property (here are some tips when shopping for investment property) .

It's Always Darkest Before the Dawn

2011-06-02

There's probably never been a better time to buy an investment property. Pessimism (especially about residential real estate) has been on the rise, stoked by the media and realization that we are headed into a "double dip" recession. Sure, prices have been declining over the past year and they may continue to decline some more before eventually recovering, but if you are investing for positive cash flow, you shouldn't care about short-term value fluctuations. Just as people once believed that real estate values would continue to rise year after year, now people are beginning to believe the opposite is true - that real estate values will continue to endlessly plummet. You simply can't lose sight of the fact that underneath all of this short term volatility, there is still a cycle.

Building A Financial Fortress

Here are some positive factors to consider for residential investment property:

- Real estate provides an excellent hedge against inflation
- There are numerous tax benefits to owning investment property
- If you are a contrarian investor, you have to start liking residential real estate (since everyone hates it now)
- Most other asset classes, including commodities, stocks and bonds are not really a bargain anymore, having increased in value significantly since the depths of the Great Recession
- People will always need somewhere to live and we are turning into a nation of renters due to inability or unwillingness to buy a home, which bodes well for owners of rental property
- Cost of capital is very attractive - you can now get a 5% (or so) 30-year fixed mortgage on non-owner-occupied property

Residential Property For Investment

2011-03-27

Now might be an excellent opportunity to buy residential property to operate as a rental.

Single family homes, condominium units and small (4 units or less) apartment buildings are looking to be very attractive long-term investments for several reasons:

- All of these types of properties can qualify for conventional 30-year fixed loans, which may not be around for very long (or not available on favorable terms) if the government is successful in abolishing Fannie Mae and Freddie Mac as they have indicated.
- Home prices are low and are continuing to fall in many areas.
- Interest rates are still very low by historical standards (check the bottom of the blog for the latest Freddie Mac interest rate survey).
- Demand for rental units will continue to be strong as the economy recovers.

- Many people don't want to or can't buy a home but still need a place to live, which makes for the perfect opportunity to invest in residential property and convert to rental use.

The most important thing to remember is that <u>cash flow</u> is king:

- When reviewing property listings, do a careful analysis of the monthly cash inflows and outflows based on realistic (slightly below-market) rent and slightly higher operating expenses.
- I use <u>Craigslist</u> to research rental rates
- If there isn't positive cash flow with conservative financial projections, don't buy the property - move on.
- Also, you need to make a careful investigation of the property to make sure you are aware of all of the issues and also what the cost will be to fix-up the property to get it into shape to rent.
- You'll also need to plan for repairs and maintenance after you own the property and include that in your cash flow budget.
- Make sure you have a good <u>real estate agent</u> who understands investment property (even better if they own a few themselves) and can write an offer quickly - this is especially important when dealing with banks
- Be prepared to pay 25% to 30% down, depending on lender requirements
- Also consider using a property manager if the monthly cash flow allows - unless you want to fix leaky faucets and change light bulbs yourself

Finding a Good Investment Property

2011-03-29

There are many great online resources to find investment properties. Listingbook is a tool that you can join for free (it used to only be available through a real estate agent). You can quickly configure Listingbook to send you a daily feed of available properties that meet your specific criteria (price, bedroom count, location, etc). Redfin is also a great site that you can join for free and will also send you a daily feed of listings that meet your preset criteria. I think the information that Redfin provides on each property and the layout is excellent and includes sale history, public record data including property tax records, comparable sales, market data, and information on schools and community amenities. If you are working with a real estate agent, they can also send custom MLS reports to you each time a new listing is posted that meets your preset criteria. I highly recommend working with a good agent who understands investment property (preferably owns a few properties him/her self).

If you subscribe to a few different sites, you can get a good sense of the market on a daily basis by scanning your email. If you see an interesting listing, you can send along to your agent to get additional information so you can run the numbers to see if it's worth making an offer.

10 Things to Remember When Looking for Investment Real Property

2012-07-29

)

With the market clearing in many areas of the US and interest rates continuing to fall to record lows, many people are thinking seriously about buying investment property for cash flow and long term capital appreciation.

Here are 10 things to remember when you are looking for investment property:

1. **Positive cash flow** - Make sure when you run all the numbers that you can have positive cash flow each and every month; otherwise, you are gambling on appreciation that may not come as quickly as you would like
2. **You won't live there** - Just because it's not something you would want to personally live in doesn't mean it's a bad investment property; you need to put your personal preferences aside and look at the numbers
3. Location, location, location - The ideal property should be close to shopping, public transportation, jobs and recreation facilities in order for it to be a good rental; sometimes you have to pay a little more to get a superior location

Building A Financial Fortress

4. **Be very careful with condos** - If you are buying a condo, make sure you read all of the condo association documents carefully and ask lots of questions - Is the association in good financial shape? Do they have a history of special assessments? Are they involved in litigation? Are they putting enough away for repair/replacement reserves? Do they have enough owner-occupants and a low enough dues delinquency rate to not cause a problem getting a loan? Where does your responsibility to maintain your unit end and the association's begin?

5. **Inspect the property** - Unless you happen to be a general contractor or expert in the building industry, don't buy a property without getting a third party inspection

6. **Factor in below-market rent and vacancy into your cash flow** - Tenant turnover is a fact of life and getting good long-term tenants is always easier if your rent is slightly below market; make sure you factor these in to your cash flow projections - check Craigslist to see what other landlords are asking in the area

7. **Have a property management strategy** - Whether you plan to manage the property yourself or hire a property manager, you should have a strategy well before you buy; if you decide to go with a property manager, make sure you interview two or three different companies early and pick the one that you think will work best for you - fees can be as much as 10% of the monthly rent

8. **Know your market and niche** - Pull out a map and draw a boundary around the area that you think will yield the best rental property - focus your search in that area; Are you looking for a 4-plex? Attached condo? Single family detached conventional home? Know what you are looking for and focus on a specific area and type of property. If it's your first investment property, it's easier to find something that's a reasonable driving distance from where you live.

9. **Use a knowledgeable real estate agent** - If you don't have a real estate license and need to use an agent, make sure your agent is experienced, understands the area and owns rental property themselves and also understands that business.

10. **Bid carefully** - Carefully review the comparable sales; then, unless the seller's asking price is ridiculous, if you are in a market that has limited supply and is getting more competitive, it's best to offer full price and be flexible on terms (i.e., cooperation with 1031 exchange, seller lease-

Building A Financial Fortress

back, closing date, etc.); trying to get a lower price for a few thousand dollars could lose the deal, especially if you are trying to buy a foreclosure or short sale and/or if you are not planning to go all cash

149 | P a g e

Buying Investment Property - Research and Inspections

2011-04-05

If you are interested in making an offer on an investment property, your goal should be to learn as much as possible about the property before you make the offer. There are a number of free online resources, including Redfin.com, Zillow.com and other sites where you can get sales history, property tax data, and information on comparable sales, etc. Your real estate agent may also have knowledge of the area or be able to help you obtain sale/lease comparables and property reports prepared by title companies/other information providers. Property reports are based on public record searches and include mortgage history, owner of record history, foreclosure status, etc.

With all the competition in the market today, your best bet is the "shotgun approach," where you submit offers on multiple properties. You will need an agent who is technologically savvy and can process offers electronically (using Docusign or similar technology) to do this. Also, you do need to do your research to evaluate comparable properties to develop an offer price. The more you try the better your chances are of landing a good one.

Once you are in escrow, you need to quickly learn as much as possible about the

Building A Financial Fortress

property to make an informed decision to continue with the purchase before your right to cancel the contract expires at the end of the inspection period (17 days in a standard California Association of Realtors form):

1. First, make arrangements to view the property with your agent - you may not have had time to view the property before you made the offer, since it may take many offers to get a property into escrow. You should be able to quickly assess whether it is worth continuing or better to cancel the escrow.
2. Review all publicly available information about the property, including information on the real estate websites, property tax records, Google search, etc. Walk around the neighborhood and talk to the neighbors.
3. Location, location location - If you are afraid to get out of your car, you might not want to buy there; however, a good rental property is not necessarily somewhere you would want to live - it just needs to work financially for you
4. Carefully review rental comp's on Craigslist and what your agent provides you from the MLS - don't be overly optimistic about rent and do assume a discount to market; it's a lot cheaper to discount the rent than it is to endure months of vacancies while you test the market
5. Next, check with your banker to make sure there are no issues with the property that would preclude getting a loan. Be especially careful of condos - lender requirements have become very stringent for these types of properties. For example, owner-occupants must make up 51% or more of the total units in the project and Fannie Mae, Freddie Mac, and FHA won't guarantee loans in condominiums where more than 15% of the home owners are 30 days or more overdue on home owners association fees.
6. If it looks good, I recommend a professional inspection of the property. The inspection report can help highlight areas of concern that you might have missed and also provides a "to do" list of repairs that may be required prior to being able to rent the property. Make sure you budget funds to do the initial repairs/renovations and plan to get them done quickly so you can start showing the property to prospective renters as soon as possible.

7. If you are buying a condo, perhaps the most important information is provided by the <u>Homeowners' Association</u>. Carefully review meeting minutes, <u>CC</u>R's, HOA budget and audit report and also the statistics on <u>owner-occupancy</u> percentage as well as delinquency rate. Ideally, you want an HOA that does not have litigation, is financially strong and does not have a history of special assessments or dramatic increases in monthly HOA dues.

8. Check in with your insurance agent for a <u>rental property</u> rate quote - maintaining adequate insurance on the property is critical; especially liability coverage - you may want to have excess coverage in an umbrella liability policy.

9. Update your <u>cash flow</u> projections to make sure that the numbers still make sense. Keep updating and reviewing the numbers as you get additional information.

10. If you don't have positive cash flow, look for another property. Don't bet on appreciation saving the day.

Fannie Mae Refinancing Rules for 5+ Financed Properties

2012-08-02

You may not be aware of this, but there are special rules governing the purchase or refinancing of investment properties when you have more than 4 properties (up to 10) with a mortgage:

1. Initial purchase of property (single unit) requires a 25% down payment (75% loan to value ratio)
2. Initial purchase of property (2-4 unit) requires a **30%** down payment (70% loan to value ratio)
3. Refinancing (limited cash out - no more than $2,000 provided at closing) of investment property requires **30%** equity (70% loan to value ratio)
4. Credit score minimum is 720

Best to talk to your lender and carefully go through all the criteria before getting too far down the path of refinancing. Doing a HARP refinancing may be an option - confirm with your lender.

Investment Property Refinancing Under HARP2

2012-06-17

If you currently own an investment property and would like to refinance to a lower rate, but the property value has declined to the point where you would have to put in a lot of additional cash in order to close, you should look into HARP2 by talking to your current lender to see if you qualify. The program is currently scheduled to end on December 31, 2013.

You may be eligible for HARP if you meet all of the following criteria:

- The mortgage must be owned or guaranteed by Freddie Mac or Fannie Mae.
- The mortgage must have been sold to Fannie Mae or Freddie Mac on or before May 31, 2009.
- The mortgage cannot have been refinanced under HARP previously unless it is a Fannie Mae loan that was refinanced under HARP from March-May, 2009.
- The current loan-to-value (LTV) ratio must be greater than 80%.
- The borrower must be current on the mortgage at the time of the refinance, with a good payment history in the past 12 months.

Maximize Cash Flow on Investment Property

2013-02-17

If you own investment property, you know that positive cash flow is very important. Ideally, when you initially purchase the property, you enjoy positive cash flow at the outset. However, in some coastal markets you may end up with a property that breaks even or is slightly negative at first and so you need to work harder to get there.

Here is a list of ideas to improve investment property cash flow:

1) Raise the rent

- Landlords are gaining in many markets as the economy covers and housing supply is constrained and you should be no different
- Keep the increases modest (i.e., 2-3 percent annually) and it will be harder for tenants to want to move
- If you have a vacancy, be sure to price up as close as you can to market when re-leasing

2) Refinance

- If you haven't already done so, refinancing is an easy way to improve monthly cash flow
- Some investment property is eligible for government programs (i.e., HARP) where loan to value ratio would not otherwise allow for a refinancing
- If you purchased recently you may have to wait to build more equity since investment property can be purchased with 25% down but refinancing requires 30% equity

4) Review liability insurance

- Periodically check the market for insurance to see if you can get a lower rate on liability insurance
- While you are at it, make sure your coverage is adequate

5) Evaluate property manager

- Check your property management company against the market - are they competitive in their fee structure?
- Are you happy with their performance?
- Get a few quotes and talk to some other companies

6) Preventive maintenance

- Make sure repairs, leaks and other issues are addressed immediately
- A few dollars spent today on preventive maintenance will save you bigger dollars down the road
- Get a few quotes before doing the work - as the economy recovers, contractors are getting busier now and are able to raise their prices

7) Other service providers

- Periodically check the market for other service providers, such as landscape maintenance

8) Review property taxes

- If the value of your property has declined since you purchased it, you may be able to appeal the value and thereby reduce your taxes
- Many jurisdictions have done this automatically in recent years but you should verify

Is Now a Good Time to Sell Real Estate? It Depends.

2011-09-08

Many are recommending that now is the time to buy real estate due to the low interest rates and collapsed values. There is also the notion that real estate provides a hedge against potential future inflation. See chart below which depicts inflation-adjusted values of US house prices over time. It may make sense to purchase a new investment property if you can get the right price, positive cash flow and lock-in a low 30-year fixed rate. However, if you currently own an investment property that doesn't cash flow, you might consider selling now. This is particularly true if any of your mortgage debt has a variable rate. If we have a significant bout of inflation in the future (the result of current Fed "money printing" - monetary policy which is highly inflationary), you could be in a situation where you are selling into a market that is further depressed due to higher interest rates (which reduce affordability and therefore demand) while your monthly negative cash flow worsens. Selling now has the advantage of liberating you from the monthly negative cash flow and protecting you from further downside risk in the event of possible further decline in value or the effect of rising interest rates and monthly payments on variable rate debt. If you have any equity in the property, it allows you to redeploy that capital to another use - perhaps cash or gold.

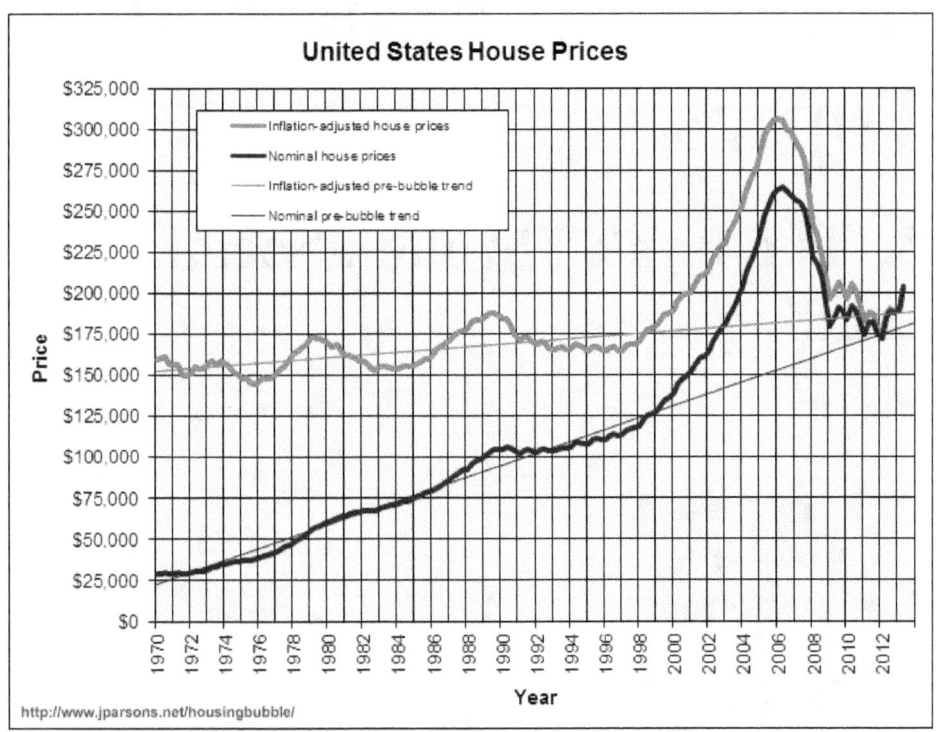

Appendix – Other Important Financial Topics

Be The Bank Through Social Lending

2011-03-27

Have you ever wanted to be a bank and borrow money at a low <u>rate of interest</u> and lend the same money at a higher rate of interest, thus earning a "spread" on the money while having no net capital <u>outlay</u>?

Building A Financial Fortress

One possibility (depending on your credit score) is to use one of the social lending sites such as Prosper.com. The way it works is you become a member of the site and first borrow money (up to $25,000 on Prosper). Once the loan funds, you then sign up to become an investor on the site and invest in a group of loans (usually $50 to $100 per loan) - Prosper has an automated bid platform that does all the work for you. Sometimes, due to a shortage of lenders, the site offers cash incentives to investors. The investor interest rates are quoted net of estimated losses, so as long as the net interest rate (after charge-offs) exceeds your cost of borrowing, you are making money on the deal. Recognize that a higher rate of interest (lower credit quality) comes with a higher risk of default, but that can be reduced by spreading the investment over many loans and over many different credit quality groups.

Since you are basically investing in consumer loans, a recovering economy is a great environment for this asset class. There's a reason why you get so many credit card offers in the mail each week (which, by the way represent a huge identity theft risk to you - you might want to read my post on this topic). Banks make a ton of money in this business, especially on late fees!

Inside Job - A Fascinating Documentary of the Global Financial Crisis

2011-05-01

If you are into documentaries and have an interest in how the Global Financial Crisis was brought about, I highly recommend watching the movie "Inside Job." It highlights the fascinating linkage between the financial services industry, the U.S. government and academia and the criminal behavior of the largest financial institutions. It also does a good job of explaining the unregulated derivatives market in layman's terms, with simple graphics. I also liked how recent current events were incorporated into the story. I have read a few books on the crisis, including The Big Short and Too Big to Fail and I think this movie does a decent job of telling the story in all its mind-numbing complexity. After watching this movie, I understand why some call them "banksters."

Are You Ready for the Aftershock?

2011-08-28

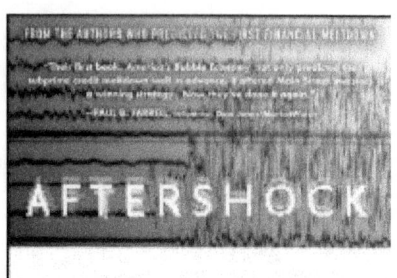

I recently read "Aftershock" by David and Robert Wiedemer and Cindy Spitzer, which I would add to my recommended reading list. In the book, the authors lay out the case for what lies ahead as the dollar bubble and government debt bubble begin to burst (the last two bubbles in our so-called "bubble economy").

When these bubbles burst, the authors claim that there are only two main asset classes that you should be invested in: cash and gold - mostly gold. All other asset classes, including stock, bonds, real estate, whole life insurance policies, etc. will suffer significant declines in value.

Building A Financial Fortress

There may well be very good values in these asset classes at some point in the future, but only after the bubbles have burst. At the core of their concern is the Federal Reserve printing money to try to stimulate the economy - they believe this is highly inflationary and that in the next one to three years, we could see very high rates of inflation - perhaps as much as 10% per year.

I was a little surprised to see real estate included in the "avoid" category. While I can understand the argument as it relates to primary residence and second home (these are really liabilities since they do not put cash into your pocket), I have long believed that investment property that provides positive cash flow would weather an inflationary storm pretty well, since the value of the asset should increase (at least in nominal dollars) and the largest cash outflow (the mortgage payment) is fixed while rent and other expenses would float up with inflation.

The recent sell-off in the stock market and downgrade of US government debt by S&P adds to the credibility of their argument that there really has been no economic recovery since the Great Recession and the stock market increase can be almost entirely attributed to the money printing operations of the Federal Reserve (which include keeping interest rates very low and quantitative easing).

There is a strong likelihood in the current weak economic environment that the government will continue to apply fiscal stimulus (further inflating the government debt bubble) and that the Federal Reserve will continue to apply monetary easing (further inflating the dollar bubble). Both of these will be intended to stimulate economic recovery, but as the Aftershock authors correctly point out, the cure will become the poison in the form of inflation.

Ironically, the "safe haven" investment of choice is US government debt each time the stock market sell-off, but that may soon change to gold (and to a lesser extent the other precious metals) when inflation becomes more significant.

Is Your Identity Safe?

2012-06-24

)

If you work hard for your money, the last thing you need is to be robbed. In our modern information society, thieves no longer have to rob you face to face. Identity theft is a growing problem. It is the fastest growing crime in the United States over the past four years - an identity is stolen every two seconds. All an identity thief needs is your name, date of birth, social security number, home address, a fake picture i.d. and they can do any of the following in your name:

- Open up credit accounts to steal goods/services, ruining your credit in the process
- Steal money from your bank accounts
- Steal your healthcare insurance coverage, potentially jeopardizing your future medical coverage and care
- Steal your social security benefits
- Apply for a job
- Commit a crime

A bad credit history can make it difficult to rent an apartment, get a job or purchase a home (or anything else on credit). In today's economy your personal information is out there at banks, credit card companies, your employer, and is always at risk of being stolen as a result of a data breach. If you apply for mortgages, you have to provide tax returns and other personal information that can also include information about your children (social security numbers, home address).

Thieves can steal personal information out of your mailbox or the trash, which is why your mailbox should be locked and you should shred any junk mail. Unsolicited credit card offers received in the mail are a common source of identity fraud, which is why it is recommended that you "opt out" of credit card offers altogether.

There are several identity theft prevention companies out there that provide monitoring/protection services including credit report activity, bank and credit card accounts, internet "black market" sites where personal information is traded, support for "opting out" of credit card offers, public records, etc. You also have an option to pay a small fee to each of the big three credit reporting companies (Experian, TransUnion and Equifax) to completely "lock down" your credit, if you want to.

This website compares several of the top identity theft prevention companies. A few dollars per month and a few minutes of your time to setup the monitoring is well worth the effort.

The average person spends more than $3,000 and 500 hours to repair the damage caused by identity theft. If your child's identity is stolen, you may not know about it for years, until they open a credit card or other financial account.

Wealth Quotes

2012-09-01

Wealth is like <u>sea-water</u>; the more we drink, the thirstier we become; and the same is true of fame.

<u>Arthur Schopenhauer | Wealth</u>

For many men, the acquisition of <u>wealth</u> does not end their troubles, it only changes them.

<u>Seneca – Wealth</u>

It is the interest of the commercial world that wealth should be found everywhere.

<u>Wealth – Edmund Burke</u>

Give me the poverty that enjoys true wealth.

<u>Henry David Thoreau – Poverty, Wealth</u>

A man is rich in proportion to the number of things he can afford to let alone.

<u>Henry David Thoreau – Wealth</u>

Books are the treasured wealth of the world and the fit inheritance of generations and nations.

<u>Henry David Thoreau – Book, Wealth</u>

Early to bed and early to rise, makes a man happy wealthy and wise.

<u>Benjamin Franklin – Wealth and wise</u>

Building A Financial Fortress

We have no more right to consume happiness without producing it than to consume wealth without producing it.

George Bernard Shaw – Happiness, Wealth

What right have you to take the word wealth, which originally meant "well-being," and degrade and narrow it by confining it to certain sorts of material objects measured by money?

John Ruskin – Wealth

Every gold piece you save is a slave to work for you. Every copper it earns is its child that also can earn for you. If you would become wealthy, then what you save must earn, and its children must earn, that all may help to give to you the abundance you crave.

Wealth and work

Wealth, like a tree, grows from a tiny seed. The first copper you save is the seed from which your tree of wealth shall grow. The sooner you plant that seed the sooner shall the tree grow. And the more faithfully you nourish and water that tree with consistent savings, the sooner may your bask in contentment beneath its shade.

Tree of wealth

[...] you have learned your lessons well. You first learned to live upon less than you could earn. Next you learned to seek advice from those who were competent through their own experiences to give it. And, lastly, you have learned to make gold work for you.

Learning the lessons

Success and Character - John Wooden

2012-09-02

These are a few of my favorite John Wooden quotes:

Things turn out best for the people who make the best of the way things turn out.
John Wooden

Success comes from knowing that you did your best to become the best that you are capable of becoming.
John Wooden

Be more concerned with your character than your reputation, because your character is what you really are, while your reputation is merely what others think you are.
John Wooden

Back to School - Now Where Can Kids Get a Financial Education?

2012-09-03

One thing is for sure, school doesn't teach kids the basics of <u>financial education</u>, which include saving, controlling spending with a budget, the difference between "<u>good debt</u>" and "<u>bad debt</u>," investing, making your money work for you instead of you working for your money, etc.

For a basic book about financial education that's also very motivational, I like <u>Rich Dad, Poor Dad</u>, a book by <u>Robert Kiyosaki</u> (I grew up in <u>Hawaii</u>, so I can relate to a lot of what he talks about in the book). It's a pretty easy read and has some great basic concepts in it.

Building A Financial Fortress

Since my son is going into 6th grade next year and is pretty good with numbers (main interest is sports statistics - all sports), I wanted to make sure I started his financial education. I made a deal with him at the beginning of the summer that I would pay him one Silver Eagle bullion coin (current estimated value about $40) if he reads the book this summer. Summer's almost over and he's only half way through. I'm not disappointed because I know he will finish it. Also, he must be learning something, because he knows the value of silver went up over the summer, so the longer he waits to finish the book, the more the coin will be worth. He has also been asking me about investments and has taken more of an interest in our household budget. Unfortunately, he still wants $100+ basketball shoes. Oh, well.

It's a good start, anyway.

Don't Quit

2012-12-28

I'm sharing this poem that my grandfather gave me when I was a kid. Not sure who the author is.

It says a lot in a very simple way and applies to investing and life:

Don't Quit

When things go wrong, as they sometimes will,
When the road you're trudging seems all uphill,
When the funds are low and the debts are high,
And you want to smile, but you have to sigh,
When care is pressing you down a bit-
Rest if you must, but don't you quit.

Life is queer with its twists and turns,
As every one of us sometimes learns,
And many a fellow turns about
When he might have won had he stuck it out.
Don't give up though the pace seems slow-
You may succeed with another blow.

Often the goal is nearer than
It seems to a faint and faltering man;
Often the struggler has given up
When he might have captured the victor's cup,
And he learned too late when the night came down
How close he was to the golden crown.

Success is failure turned inside out-
The silver tint of the clouds of doubt,
And you never can tell how close you are,
It may be near when it seems afar;
So stick to the fight when you're hardest hit,-
It's when things seem worst that you mustn't quit.

Acknowledgements

- Charts presented throughout, as noted, are courtesy of www.shadowstats.com (Shadow Government Statistics)
- Photo credits:
  - Kevindean
  - 401(k) 2012
  - Wvhomes
  - Wikipedia
  - Paolo Camera
  - Tax Credits
  - LendingMemo
  - Bransorem
  - Adkorte
  - R0b0r0b
  - Sprottmoney
  - GGtimeshares
  - Alan Cleaver
  - Markyeg
  - Woodleywonderworks
  - Ingot

Other Books

If you enjoyed this book, please consider reading my follow-on book in the series on real estate investing: **Building a Financial Fortress: Getting Started in Real Estate Investing**

www.ingramcontent.com/pod-product-compliance
Lightning Source LLC
Chambersburg PA
CBHW051505170526
45166CB00001B/402